Connecting to *Beautiful*

A Journey from Disabled Child to Wholehearted Woman

DEB DRAKE

Graphics and cover by Kelly Teno of Truce Creative.

Literary consulting services and developmental editing provided by Clara Rose of RoseDale Communications. Published by RoseDale Publishing, an imprint of RoseDale Communications, Inc.

ISBN: 9780997512083

Praise for Connecting to Beautiful

A debut memoir recounts a woman's efforts to overcome physical pain and depression, eventually finding her way to a positive self-image.

Drake's mother's health was compromised by juvenile diabetes, which caused serious difficulties in her pregnancy. When the author was born in the 1960s, three months premature, she weighed only 4 pounds; she was not expected to survive. She was diagnosed with cerebral palsy, and her parents were told she "would be intellectually impaired" and "might need to be institutionalized." But with the aid of leg braces for 10 years, surgery when she was 12, and physiotherapy, Drake was able to walk on her own (albeit with a limp), attend school, and lead a fulfilling life as an occupational therapist. Now in her 50s, she recently married. Her childhood was complicated not only by her own disability, but by her mother's illness and her parents' deteriorating marriage as well. She recalls understanding at an early age that she should not cause her mother any stress, which could disrupt her blood sugar levels and cause a diabetic coma: "I learned to not be a burden. I learned to be quiet. I learned to play outside. I learned to not be in the way." She also learned to think of herself as unworthy: "I carried such damaging shame; I believed in my inferiority, my brokenness, my separateness." The author's descriptive prose portrays the agony she endured each morning during her childhood when she strapped on her metal leg braces; her intense feelings of loneliness as she searched for love in all the wrong places; her 10-year bout with bulimia that landed her in the hospital; and more. Ultimately, she explains, it was through her love for her disabled patients that she began to fill the empty spaces in her heart: "I found a reason for being." The narrative… remains a remarkable story of strength and determination.

Honest, informative, and emotional; an inspirational affirmation of "the value, depth, and beauty" of the disabled that challenges stereotypes.

- Kirkus Reviews

Foreword

In *Connecting to Beautiful* Debra Drake takes you on a heartfelt and sincere journey as she uses her connections to art, music, books, nature, and people to seek her own path to *Beautiful*.

I first met Debra about 30 years ago when she became an occupational therapy student. In my memories of that time, I recall her sitting in my office telling me, among other things, she had cerebral palsy. Upon reading her book so many years later, I realized that I had never considered Debra to be disabled. Sure, I knew she had a limp, but my perception of her was a bright, well-spoken, and self-assured young woman who would certainly be able to succeed in OT school.

Reading about her journey made me realize how limited my view had been. Debra provides an intimate view into her sometimes turbulent life while confronting various life challenges. For many readers, memories of middle school (or junior high for us older folks) may immediately come to mind since anyone who was the least bit different was always teased and tormented. Imagine going through that with a disability.

Debra provides insight into how she dealt with the cycle of self-disgust and self-destruction, her feelings of shame, and her own body perception over all stages of her life. How does one reach the goals of feeling self-love, trust, hope, empathy, self-confidence and purpose? Fortunately, Debra has shared her process with us, and shown how she traveled the road to *Beautiful*.

- Susan Heling Kaplan, PhD, MBA, OT

<u>Dedication</u>

Thank you, Mary, for showing me a door
where all I saw was a wall.

Table of Contents

CONNECTING TO BEAUTIFUL

Acknowledgments

This book would not have been written were it not for my mother in law Mary.

She led me to think about the effects of Alzheimer's, the need for stories to build connections to others, and the drive to leave something worthwhile behind.

I also wish to thank Sarah, who guided this memoir by reminding me of the importance of passion.

My editor and publisher, Clara Rose at RoseDale Communications, stood by my side even while I was hitting the DELETE button and trashing the first draft.

I give thanks for all the therapists I've worked with through the years but especially Susan Kaplan for asking me to begin my writing career, helping contribute to her magazine, Occupational Therapy in Mental Health, so so many years ago.

This memoir is my own,

filled with my memories that contain errors,

misperceptions, and timeline discrepancies;

what can I say? The mind weaves its own story.

Introduction

*"From the moment a soul has the grace to
know God, she must seek."*
-   *Mother Teresa*

On the Path

Connecting to Beautiful. This is my story, the story that begins with a disabled child, growing up with shame, sorrow, fear and even self-disgust. Then growing into a caring, generous, loving and self-confident whole-hearted woman.

How do I move from being so disconnected from myself, from life, to being fully engaged and connected to Beautiful? That's beautiful with a capital B – it's transcendent, it's inspiration, it is the Divine.

What is the magic, the serendipity, that THING taking me across the bridge to fulfillment? Why, that's just Mother Nature in the form of a hurricane, that's a sweet-talking jailor, a sushi-loving gymnast, a broken-down horse, and an old Elvis tune. These are the things that led me to reach out to others, to be vulnerable, to love. And in reaching out, I let the healing in.

It's an all too common story of a somewhat broken child, physically disabled, emotionally robbed, and spiritually hollow. But this story is also filled with unexpected and transformative moments of connection to the right-ness of life, of knowing that yes, I am in the right place and this is the perfect moment to receive an acceptance of self.

I've discovered the vital, the life-giving aspects of relationships in my own healing journey and throughout my life while dealing with my own physical disability.

In discovering those healing moments, I am brought back to the truth of my interconnectedness, my relatedness, and my responsibility to others. In acknowledging this, I can receive the gifts of wisdom, sensitivity, compassion, gratitude, and grace.

This book is for all those who relate to others, to nature, to art and music, to books and words, all things created by God and Man.

My mission is to educate and inspire folks to connect with others – be they disabled, non-disabled, the friends and family of the disabled, their caregivers and other healthcare professionals, regardless of their age – be they children, teens, adults, or seniors.

My life and my story aim to reinforce the value, depth, and beauty of folks labeled as disabled. I mean to dispel the feelings of ugliness, disgust, and hatred for oneself as a person with disabilities and I seek to erase those attitudes from others.

My meandering exploration of self-discovery and healing is by no means over; however, it may show others that no-one is ever truly alone, isolated, separated, or lost. These states of separateness are illusions, cruel lies embodying the mistaken conviction that self-worth is in doubt or even absent.

Will I be a hero on this life journey? Well, if a hero is afraid, filled with shame, and suffers intermittently debilitating depression, then I guess I'm a hero in this story.

The tools in my backpack for this inner journey are a combination of people, events, animals, art, music, books, and nature, that reveal themselves in my everyday life, to change my vision of life circumstances. They are those things that assist me in acting in new ways.

What helps me realize what was once a tragedy is now seen as a moment of great change and insight? How do I become closer to others as well as the Divine within my own suffering? And exactly where is the Divine? Must I transcend myself? Or do I reach inside myself for the Divine? Am I the Divine?

These questions swirl in my mind as I write, trying to communicate the depth and breadth, of the meaningfulness of each and every moment. Simple moments that should just float by unnoticed become significant life changing events; these moments provide not only healing but also provide a direction toward my future.

These moments act as a compass and my destination is fulfillment and gratitude. My path is not linear but often meanders back on itself and leads me back to familiar feelings of self-doubt; however, with those familiar feelings comes a certainty of buried treasure leading me back to the knowledge of connectedness.

So, how do I move:

> From Shame to Vulnerability and Trust?

> From Suffering to Hope?

> From Self Destruction to Self Love?

> From Disgust to Empathy?

> From Fear to Courage?

> From Depression to Confidence and Purpose?

> From Lost to Finding Home?

Join me on this trek and maybe some of these places of fear and doubt will look familiar; but know this adventure may also lead YOU to fulfillment.

Never begin a memoir with your birth.

Apparently, that's a well-known axiom for writers and it's a good thing my book editor told me that, because I was on the way to committing this cardinal sin and boring my readers to tears.

Actually, I think the story of my birth has some entertaining moments but that will be in another chapter. I guess I will just begin with where I am right now.

At this not so tender age of 54 years, I find myself on sabbatical after thirty years of working as an occupational therapist, looking forward to a future of limited mobility complicated by my diagnoses of cerebral palsy and osteoporosis.

I now wear leg braces that I haven't needed since I was a child and I find myself reverting back to those childhood frustrations of wanting to rant and rave at life, for imprisoning me yet again.

I'm frightened of not being able to care for myself and of being a burden to my new husband. I'm fearful of not having an income. I'm fearful of not having purpose or meaning in my life.

But then, I met a book editor at a health conference.

And I knew this was where I was meant to be in my life. All those fears and doubts that were a product of the mistaken belief in my separateness from others, dissolved into mere smoke and ash in the excitement and fire of a new beginning. This ending of a familiar and routine existence has allowed a new vision of meaning to assert itself.

My new vision of myself includes being a wife, a mother, a grandmother, a cook, a seamstress, a writer, an educator, and finally an advocate for the disabled. This new vision has evolved out of the increasing limitations in my own mobility. Let me reiterate, my changing physical condition has led me to a profound change in my ability to connect with others and see myself in new ways. My physical vulnerability has been reflected now in my psyche.

To find love and connectedness requires the courage to be vulnerable, the courage to let myself leap off the mountain of familiarity, respectability, and routine, to essentially leave everything I know behind me.

I'm leaping into the ocean of my subconscious from the precipice of familiarity. My desires, my passions, and my drive swirl around me in this ocean but the shark's fin of doubt and fear slice through the waters of my inner self.

My passion for connecting with others is my lifeboat in these dark moments of discovery. But the dark moments finally release their hold on my mind, my soul, and my behavior by being brought out of the dark waters and into the light of truth. At my most vulnerable, I can find strength in the discovery of truth.

For many years, my identity revolved around the seemingly opposite roles of healer and patient. I am a disabled occupational therapist and I had been living the outward projection of my inner battles. But as you will soon discover, these so-called battles were my attempts to keep my inner healer and healing patient separated, whereas my soul seeks integration of these two halves into a magnificent whole.

Myself as healer was expressed through my work as an occupational therapist; my sense of self was intertwined with the powerful tenets of my profession. The value of being independent, self-reliant, and capable after suffering a disabling condition, such as a stroke or spinal cord injury, are paramount not only in my profession but had been in my own life as well.

My own self-worth had been so enmeshed with my own ability to be independent that this had become my burden as well as my driving force. Seeing myself as needing to be healed, was in direct contrast to my self-image as healer, or so I thought.

So much of my life consisted of trying to hide my physical pain brought on by spasticity; I couldn't let anyone know of my all-encompassing exhaustion at the end of a work day. I grew expert at placing a welcoming smile on my face, but sometimes the smile did not span the distance to my eyes.

Even as I write this, I tend to downplay the ways in which having cerebral palsy now guides my day to day decisions; it even affects how I shower or brush my teeth.

But instead of denying the need to be healed, I began experimenting with integrating my *incomplete-ness*. How does one integrate a hole into a whole? Clever question even if I do say so.

My curiosity in uniting my healer and healing self led me to question my perceptions of my life, myself, and my values. I've reassessed these values and concluded that, yes, being independent is significant; however, it's the ability to connect with others that gives life most meaning.

Those events in my life that I had seen as significant tragedies are now re-framed with the knowledge of our interconnectedness with not only the hearts of each other, but with the beauty and power of nature, the joy and angst of art, the meaning and drive of work, and the ebullience and exuberance of play.

I can see my life now as I would read a book, incomplete certainly but open and vulnerable, with hidden and not so hidden meanings, spell-binding, but with a cohesiveness of a most beloved story.

I won't write about my birth yet because that is simply not allowed but I will begin with stories to help illustrate my relationships with my parents.

Daddy's Little Girl?

My father and I have a strained relationship; each one of us tries to connect with the other but we seem to fly off in different directions when we get close to each other, like magnets with the same polarity.

When the phone rings and I see that he is calling me, I'm unable to pick up the phone right away, as thoughts fly through my head like supersonic birds. Is he calling me because the news won't be on for another 10 minutes? Is he calling from a doctor's waiting room in which his appointment is scheduled 10 minutes from now? Is he in the garage on the way to his car? Because we both know he can't talk while driving. Hmm.

After these bitter thoughts come and go, I remind myself that he did indeed initiate contact with me, that he wants to make a connection. I remind myself of the days he took me to daycare on the back of his motorcycle (with a stuffed pink bear strapped down behind us). I smile and then I can call him back and we speak to each other with well-rehearsed lines.

We speak about inconsequential things, the weather, my car, my job and although I initially respond to his comments as criticism, I realize that he needs to be needed.

He reminds me with each phone call that I need to check the air pressure in my tires, although he knows my car has a sensor for this, and that I need to watch my weight because being overweight and OLD is no picnic.

I suppose his comments may be called passive-aggressive but I chose to think of them as being cries in the wilderness, cries to reconnect with his need to be a daddy. He's not able to meet my needs as a grown daughter but some days I chose to forget that and let a little foolish hope in my heart.

Even without a healthy give and take, my respect for

him has grown, as I've come to realize that my parents' marriage stayed intact until I graduated from high school, just as his own parents had chosen to remain married until he graduated from high school.

For many years I was angry at him for prolonging their unhappy marriage until I realized what a profound gift my parents had given me; they showed me what commitment and sacrifice looked like even if I saw their sacrifices as unnecessary. I saw the wounds and imperfections of my parents, but I also saw them striving to re-make themselves and their lives after I had grown.

I have an old photograph of my father; it shows him in his early twenties, handsome as all get out, in full 1960's Jacques Cousteau-like scuba gear on an empty, rocky beach in the Mediterranean, with startlingly blue skies, just like my dad's eyes. Maybe the vibrant blues were because it was Kodachrome, but that just makes this photo better.

It's inconceivable to me that this virile and vigorous man would sire a peanut-like (4 lb.) disabled child. I keep this picture of him because I can see the dare-devil, rock star, James Bond quality in him and I pray that part of him hopefully is somewhere deep inside me. Because that courage and that daring lay the foundation for a whole-hearted life.

My father had a significant bout with cancer (when isn't cancer significant?) about seven years ago and since he has been in remission, I've been looking forward to his inevitable re-evaluation of his own life. I've been eager to see his recognition of the importance of relationships, to develop the ability to gather others to him rather than suffer the anxieties of not being wealthy enough or handsome enough or fit enough.

Sadly, what I had believed to be the inevitable has not occurred. I remind myself to cherish him as I cherish my own blossoming of self.

Like Mother, Like Daughter

Writing about my mom is much more difficult than I expected; I had somehow believed that because my mom has been dead for over twenty years, that I could easily explain all my feelings for her in a few paragraphs. But this isn't easy at all.

I'm certain that I got my love for all things medical from her. Between the ages of seven and twelve, I would sneak into my parents' bedroom; I had discovered this wondrous treasure of medical textbooks hidden in the bottom drawer of my mom's nightstand.

I would crawl into their bedroom, keeping my head down and hiding on the side of the bed furthest from the door. I would lean my back against the nightstand, with the drawer handle digging into my back, and read those yellowing tomes as they rested in my lap, too heavy to lift.

Those books must have been at least twelve to fifteen years old because my mom went to nursing school when she was sixteen. But her Juvenile Diabetes interfered with her schooling, her career as a nurse, and ultimately led to her early death.

Not only did her JD interfere with her school and work, it affected her ability to carry a child, (me) to full term. She had me three months early and in the 1960's that was significant to both mother and child.

She was at great risk if she attempted to get pregnant in the future and I was not expected to survive. So, my folks decided to get a life insurance policy for me to pay for the funeral and they also decided I didn't need any siblings on the outside chance that I did survive.

I was later diagnosed with cerebral palsy; my folks were told I would be intellectually impaired and that I might need to be institutionalized.

I survived, and I wasn't institutionalized but my mother's frequent hospitalizations affected our family life; there was a constant tension in the air, almost like the low humming of a refrigerator.

We were all hyper vigilant and aware of the fragility of my mother's life. All her activities, including cooking, cleaning, or playing with me, could send her blood sugar levels plummeting like a bird shot from the sky. She could go into a deadly diabetic coma at any time; those comas were frequent and gave little warning of their approach.

We learned to mobilize our resources, recognize the

signs and symptoms of high or low blood sugar and act accordingly. We modified our lifestyle to allow for quick access to a hospital but most importantly I learned to *not be a burden*. I learned to be quiet. I learned to play outside. I learned to not be in the way.

I won't say that I necessarily became more nurturing and solicitous of my mother, but I did learn the value of being independent and able to care for myself.

I did the unforgivable and wrote about my birth in the introduction, but now I can show you how I moved from the desert and loneliness of shame to a life-giving oasis of trust.

Chapter 1

From Shame to Trust and Vulnerability

Last night as I was sleeping,
I dreamt-marvelous error!
That I had a beehive there inside my heart.
And the golden bees
were making white combs
And sweet honey
From my old failures.

-Antonio Machado
(Last Night As I Was Sleeping)

Crippled. Spaz. Handicapped. Birth Defect. Botched Abortion. Deformed. Disabled. Gimp. Jerry's Kids. Vegetable. Retarded.

Those words came easily to paper; I've heard them so often that it feels like they may be tattooed on my brain.

It's not just about writing *those words*, seeing *those words*, or even hearing *those words*, it's all about owning *those words*. I carried them around with me as if they were blood sucking ticks or leeches; *those words* were soul sucking leeches.

I carried such damaging shame; I believed in my inferiority, my brokenness, my separateness.

Crippled Girl

Thinking about those leg braces, that I wore until the age of ten, brings revulsion and rage to my heart, even though it's been decades since I've worn them. The memories of the pain, the confinement, and the loss of spontaneity bring the despair back to me so sharply that I must instruct myself to take calming breaths.

To wear leg braces, I had to strap myself into my own prison; tough leather and metal buckles are made for a straight-jacket or the electric chair, and don't belong on a child, especially not me. The outside frame of my leg braces acted as the cage, imprisoning my frail bird like legs, holding them still and allowing the weight of my body to rest on my hips instead of the ground.

I knew the ground all too well; my trips and falls were an everyday part of my life, both with and without braces. The whoosh through the air as my head moved rapidly from a vertical to a horizontal position, the too-late response of my arms trying to slow my fall but ending up tangled beneath me. The taste of dirt and Saint Augustine grass in my mouth, the needle-like stinging of my palms and knees, the struggle to take a deep breath after the air had been pushed out of my lungs by my own body weight, and the resigned discouragement that this had happened yet again. All a part of my day.

It hurt to wear leg braces, my legs and feet being forced to move in foreign and unknown ways. *I can't move this way!* I would scream inside my head. Tears trying to escape my eyes and run down my face, my tears could run but I could not

Crazy Legs

Crazy Legs, now that nickname, I can live with. It puts a goofy grin on my face and my heart feels bubbly. Who knew that a coworker's warped sense of humor and that silly nickname could banish shame?

Crazy legs became a passport to join my fellow coworkers in the day to day frustrations, as well as the unexpected miracles of being on a rehabilitation unit. When a nickname allows for inclusion in the group, the illusion of separateness dissolves like bubbles in a glass of champagne, leaving only the sweet taste of belonging behind.

This wasn't a group of people set out to identify me as crippled, as less than, as incapable, but rather this was a group of folks who were inclusive of all, recognizing differences but valuing strengths. That's what we call a team.

I had a wonderful boss who recognized my ability to connect with and treat my patients in a way that other able-bodied therapists might not be capable of doing. I basked in the warm glow of his attention and appreciation. That warmth called forth a flower of self-acceptance and trust, in not only myself but the supportive group of people around me.

I was in a work setting in which my physical

limitations were actually valued as a unique part of not only myself, but the department as a whole. I could easily uncover the frustrations that physical impairments brought to our rehabilitation patients, those related to a loss of self-identity that can accompany a disabling condition.

Being appreciated for my insight and the therapeutic use of myself as a tool for change was like rain to a thirsty flower. Such an outpouring of compassion couldn't help but fill me with joy and displace my shame.

Eating My Heart Out

Growing up, our household's relationship to food was unique in that my mother followed a strict diabetic diet and my father followed an equally strict diet due to his demanding body building hobby. These diets focused on plain, dry chicken, lots of flavorless vegetables, and fruit. My folks limited all the satisfying foods such as bread, potatoes, or corn and they eliminated all junk foods and sweets. Therefore, I eagerly awaited the summers that involved visiting my grandparents' home.

My grandparents taught me the adult sophistication of drinking burning hot coffee, while I struggled to not grimace at the bitterness of it. I would hold back a yelp of pain as it scalded the roof of my mouth. They showed me the simple joys of dunking donuts in that black, bitter swirl, releasing the magic of coffee-flavored sweetness. I ate crispy, fatty, fried baloney sandwiches on mushy white bread and I savored overflowing hot chocolate sundaes from Dairy Queen.

This created a perfect storm of conflict with my father who was particularly obsessed with my weight. There were angry bribes, unresolved arguments, and crazy conversations.

"Do you want to look like that fat person over there?"

"You don't want another helping of potatoes."

"I'll give you a dollar if you do your exercises."

Those comments were a direct blow to my sense of worth and image of my body, skewed and skewered already by my cerebral palsy. It's heartbreaking and it's soul crushing, when a parent uses cruelty to control a child.

So, I began dieting, and somehow dieting led to fasting once a week, which led to fasting two and three days a week, leading then to laxative abuse, and spitting food out of my mouth at mealtimes when my folks weren't looking, and then building finally to vomiting after mealtimes occasionally and then ultimately to vomiting daily.

Later in college I would learn the name for this eating disorder. I had suffered unexpected heart problems and was hospitalized due to complications of my bulimia, yet my family seemed unaware of the underlying cause of my health problems.

I was certain that I would do more damage to my body; I couldn't stop my binging and purging. I would consume entire cakes in minutes then push three fingers down my throat, past the base of my tongue, and vomit. The rush of digested cake up the back of my throat was sweet and soothing. The splash into the toilet was comforting and I could relax after the frenzy of binging.

After much soul searching, living with this shameful compulsion, I vowed to confess this aberration to my mother during my senior year at university.

My mom was in the bathroom putting on her makeup; how appropriate that my confession should take place in the bathroom, the site of my secret purging.

I blurted out, "I eat then I vomit," I had my eyes glued to the pattern on the bathroom rug.

She responded with words I could never have anticipated, "I know."

I was frozen, I couldn't think about this. This just isn't right.

"I binged and purged for ten years after getting married; it started on my honeymoon," she continued.

Well that explains a hell of a lot, the bitter words

screamed and echoed inside my skull.

I wanted, no, I needed absolution for the sins of my shame and my bulimia. I needed forgiveness and comfort. I had come to my mother seeking solace. Instead I found more grief and anguish, enough grief that surely, I must burst wide open with it, like an overfilled garbage bag, leaking filth and stink.

Instead of parenting me, I was forced into a position to parent my mother, to comfort and protect her. But she knew better than anyone the anguish and self-hatred I felt while binging.

Why couldn't she have intervened? Why didn't she stop me? Why didn't she reach out to me as I struggled with these demons?

These questions ran unceasingly through my mind, a Times Square banner with bright lights and a never-ending scroll blaring my frustration.

I had a flash fire of anger at her apparent neglect, then, I grieved. There was a hole in my chest. I grieved for her. I grieved for myself. A black hole welcomed me with the comfort of darkness and anonymity.

I realized, with an overwhelming sadness, one that covered me like a heavy and suffocating blanket, that I needed to take care of myself and set my parents free. I needed to free them from my fiery anger, my dark sadness, and my heavy disappointment.

If I didn't set them free, I would be tied to them and to their failures, trying to run away from them, but merely dragging them behind me. I would only see them and consequently see myself as a failure. I knew this as surely as I know my name.

I saw them as fragile and quite human, with their own struggles and burdens. I saw their priorities and values as misguided, but I tried to honor their own life decisions.

I needed to delve deeper into what I had seen as catastrophic failures, and discover the meaning, the Beauty, the Divine, in those situations. And, in freeing them, I would be free to live my own life.

A Foodie is Born

After graduating from high school, I got a set of luggage from my folks, and after graduating college, I got a doll. Yes, a doll, a baby doll in fact, a lovely present but so bewildering.

Although I was hurt by the gut punch of receiving luggage, certain that my parents wanted me to leave, shame filled my body and I felt the heat in my face when I received the doll; I seemed to be a mystery to my parents. By giving me a doll, they reinforced the message that they didn't really know or understand my dreams, my priorities, my fears or my questions about life.

My shame seemed to be a fall back emotion; if I didn't know how to feel, I would just revert to shame. I knew to be gracious even if confused about this gift, because *I was raised right.*

I soon moved out of my home, renting a room in a three-bedroom house, from a stranger. It seemed like this should be such a defining moment in my budding independence, but I was just moving from one stranger's home, the home of my parents, to another stranger's home.

It seemed more of a let-down to me. Instead of the excitement and celebration of moving out, I felt my parents' sigh of relief at seeing me reach adulthood somewhat unscathed and I could hear the dim echo of them dusting their hands of me.

As an unexpected consequence of moving, I came to the realization that I was not binging and purging. Those mind obliterating frenzies of gorging, shoving and filling myself with every soft and sweet anesthetic baked good within arms-reach, just stopped. The tension, the building tsunami of anxiety, disappeared from my days with a suddenness that was a slap in my face.

I was no longer held captive by conflicts and anxieties; there were no more battlefields, no need to fight and no need to escape. I had been freed by removing myself from the immediate influence of my parents. Sadness was mixed with my joy of enlightenment; I didn't know what kind of relationship I could have with my parents moving forward.

My relationships with my parents were tentative;

however, my relationship to food blossomed like a bloomin' onion. I found good friends and good food simultaneously; we explored the richness and spice of French-Vietnamese food, the pungent freshness of Thai food, the joy of buttery-tasting sushi, the addictive power of Cuban coffee and pastries, and the list goes on and on.

I'm a self-proclaimed foodie; I love to prepare, to cook, to smell, and to taste food. Upcoming cooking classes send me into giddy anticipation of a sensory extravaganza. Don't even get me started on pizza!

I'm a bit softer and rounder now than when I was dieting, fasting, and abusing my body with binging and purging, but I'm much freer.

Moving from a severe, long-term (ten year) eating disorder, with food seen as the enemy, to my current love affair with food was brought about by the recognition that moving away from my parents was actually, moving toward my health and joy of self.

My shame in having cerebral palsy, in wearing braces, in moving differently from others, and in experiences of pain and spasticity, had a strong hold on my self-esteem.

My feelings, in living with my shameful eating disorder, affected my ability to connect with others as well as to reconnect with my sense of self. I would also experience a much different kind of shame.

Assault and (C)harming

When I was about fourteen, suffering not only the normal hormonal upheaval of being a teen, but also carrying around the fractured body image of a teen with bulimia and cerebral palsy, I found connection through the youth group at our local church.

My mom was a respected member of the church community; we had our priest and other church members, young and old, hold prayer meetings at the house.

One of our adult leaders, John, acted as ever-present assistant within the youth group and frequently drove us to events, seeing as he had a large white maintenance van to transport us all around town. He was a big guy, about 300 pounds; he looked like he could take care of himself, or us, if we were ever in trouble.

I was full of energy and excitement because I had a new outfit and we were all going out to a James Taylor concert at a fancy musical theatre in the next county over, about an hour's drive away.

I remember looking at myself in the mirror and smiling; I had put on a turquoise tank top and pristine white pants that showed my curves. Tonight, I wasn't fat, ugly, or crippled; I was pretty. No one would notice my limp, my extra fifteen pounds, or my pimples; I was looking confident and feeling it too.

I didn't think twice about it when John told me it was just the two of us going to the concert; that just meant I could sit in the passenger seat and play with the radio if I wanted. I was nearly bouncing on the seat, I was so happy.

The concert was romantic, touching, and luxurious; the seats were covered in velvet; there were chandeliers hanging from the ceiling and I knew the words to every song. I was certain that James Taylor knew I was in the audience and that he was singing to me.

I wasn't even sure if John attended the concert; I was enveloped in the sensory experience and didn't notice anyone around me that night.

I was still in that state of bliss as John and I got back in the van for the ride home. I buckled myself in and he started the engine. We chatted about music a bit, I was humming a song from the concert, when something that John said brought me up short. I stopped humming and turned to him, "What?" I asked confused, I must not have heard him right.

"I said, do you like hunting," he turned his head and smiled but his smile didn't match his question.

Why would you smile and ask me if I liked hunting, I thought but didn't say aloud, I just squinted my eyes at him.

He kept driving down the dark, isolated road as he reached over my lap to the glove compartment of the van. He reached into the glove box with his right hand and pulled out a hunting knife, a cruel looking knife, shiny even in the semi-darkness of the illuminated dashboard and radio lights.

John pulled the van onto the side of the road; we were alone. I couldn't even hear the music of crickets in fields nearby.

He said, "I can make you do anything I want with my hunting knife," and he brought the knife close to my face, so I could see and smell the heavy-duty serrated blade.

He placed the flat of the blade on my neck; it was cold against my hot neck. I could feel my pulse against the knife. I felt the heat of blood rush to the top of my head then rush hurriedly back down to my feet. I shivered with a chill.

"Get in the back of the van," he spoke while holding the knife. I unbuckled myself from the seat and crouched down so my head wouldn't hit the ceiling of the van. I was trembling; not just my arms and legs were trembling, but my stomach and back as well. My breath was trembling. My throat was dry and sore. My mind lifted out of my head, still trapped in the van but not trapped inside my skull.

"Lay down," he said. I didn't know if he was looking at me, my own gaze was on the floor. I positioned my body as if I were a toy soldier abandoned on the playground, arms at my sides, legs together, and staring upward. I kept my gaze away from the knife and away from him.

I suddenly remembered that he liked to pick his nose and eat his boogers. I felt like I would retch.

His snot-filled mouth and filthy hands would be on my pristine white pants, my new pants that I was wearing for the first time. I loved these pants, but I knew I'd never wear them again.

I was terrified of his body, his mass; he could stop me from filling my lungs with air if he put his weight on me. I wasn't able to imagine my true fear; I had never even been kissed by a boy. I couldn't imagine what rape would be.

I felt his body weigh me down, I felt his hands pushing me around. I rolled and moved as he pushed and pulled as if I were a dead child, because I was dead, truly dead.

I felt saliva on me, and sweat, and stink. He cursed and threatened as he held his knife at my neck. He insulted me, yelled at me, blamed me, hated me, and bullied me. He was frustrated by my non-action, my silence. He recognized that I had left my body behind and traveled to some safe space away from him and the van. I was sleeping on a soft cloud away from saliva on my skin, snot in my mouth, dirt on my clothes, and rusty metal grinding into my back.

He let me get up after what seemed to be hours of terror. Time seemed to stretch and compress that night, like nasty, filthy chewing gum that sticks to the sole of your brand-new white shoes.

I was alive, and I bucked myself into the passenger seat; I was numb to what the rest of the evening would bring.

He continued to hold the knife as he drove, repeating that he could do anything he wanted to me. I silently agreed; I was drained of everything; I was an insubstantial skeleton surrounded by skin, barely holding me together.

I slowly became aware of my surroundings; I felt the seat under me; I felt the cold glass on the side of my face as I rested my head against the window. I heard his threats continue like a radio set on *the Insulting Station, where we play threats and insults all night long- commercial-free.*

Then I opened my eyes and saw that we were on the turnpike. I felt my heart beat faster and my eyes open wider; I recognized this part of the turnpike. There was a tollbooth coming up in a mile or so. I could unbuckle my seatbelt, open the door and roll out as he slowed down. I could make my way to the manned tollbooth and safety. This plan could work; I could see it happening in my mind's eye. I could feel it.

I was awake, alive, and clever. John was distracted, and he was not clever. Or so I thought.

I felt the brakes engage and suddenly John reached his right arm, still holding the knife, across my body. He engaged the door lock and threatened, "I'm gonna sell your ass in Gould's if you try and leave me." I wasn't sure what that meant but my mind filled with images of being injected with heroin, of being repeatedly raped and beaten, of being abandoned and alone. I was fourteen, I was with a respected church member, and I feared for my life.

It seemed like hours later when I recognized the sight of my home through the dirty windshield. John reached across me and unlocked the door. I slowly swiveled my head to him, seeking permission to leave. He pressed the buckle release and pushed me out of the van.

I landed on the grass of the front lawn, on my hands and knees. It was wet and cool soaking through my pants; grass stuck to the palms of my hands as I watched the ugly, white van drive away.

That night was buried deep inside me for many years, like the burial of a sought-after predator, a reeking, disgusting, foul animal gladly interred and never to be brought back to life.

I would find healing in a most unlikely place, not realizing the profound changes that would occur in my life afterward.

Ride a Wild Horse

I had a dear friend whose grandson was about four years old. He was a beautiful brown-haired boy, but he suffered greatly when challenged in strange and unfamiliar environments.

He had extreme difficulty making eye contact with his family or with children his own age; this included my friend, his grandmother. He was unable to bond properly and did not form the happy relationships that a normal four-year old could experience.

He was hypersensitive to loud noises and crowds of people; he preferred the quietness of solitude. He was living a lonely life and my friend was determined to change that for him, to help him develop ties to others.

He had just been diagnosed with autism and if he was unable to bond with people, well, she would try to help him bond with animals.

A local ranch provided horse riding lessons for the disabled; this is actually called hippotherapy, and it's been a well-documented therapeutic tool in working with folks with a variety of disabling conditions.

At this ranch, I could watch this self-involved, frightened little boy reach out to touch a horse. Typically, he would run away from touching something unfamiliar, but he couldn't resist reaching out to this immense, warm, living, breathing creature.

I watched him come alive during these lessons; I saw smiles and heard laughter. Then I began to see even more; my friend's grandson began to follow directions and play games with the horse, and then finally, with others.

I was so moved by this that I spoke to the horse

trainer; I wanted to learn how to get up on a horse. I was certain that this was something I could learn.

Well, after learning how to fall in a pasture (it's a lot softer and muddier than falling on a sidewalk), the trainer decided that maybe I didn't need to bring my horse from pasture to stables. She would teach me to ride a horse already in the stables.

I explained shyly to the trainer how my cerebral palsy made it awkward to open my legs; I told her that I wasn't able to open my legs wide enough for a saddle. I was expecting resistance from her, but she quickly got a narrow-waisted horse for me; she told me he was an Arabian horse, had fewer ribs, and was thus easier to ride.

The trainer delighted in telling me the stories of all the horses on the ranch, her rescued horses, the too old or too crippled horses; they were the most gentle and considerate horses in working with the disabled.

Mine was no exception; he let me take a considerable amount of time to move my right leg over his back. I used my right arm and my trainer used both arms to help move and position my leg. I felt such amazingly indescribable joy; I was so happy I was sure that the corners of my smile touched my ears.

During the course of several lessons, my trainer challenged me to keep my hands still and guide the horse by communicating only with the muscles of my back, my hips, my legs and stomach. I could direct the horse through the movements of my body as I sat astride him; this was unbelievable.

I could feel the muscles in his back against my thighs. I could feel his ribs against my calves; I knew when he expanded his ribs to take a breath. I could close my eyes and I could feel if he had his head turned to the right or to the left. I felt the warmth of the horse up through my groin. I began to cry.

Unwelcome memories of the sexual assault came flooding back as if the thoughts were riding on the crests of my tears. In burying my memories, I hadn't set myself free, I had tied myself to a graveyard of despair. It was time to dig up these memories, bring them to the light of truth, grieve, then let them go; otherwise, I would never be free.

Shame is so isolating; it is a clever magician, turning trust into self-doubt and fear. The fear arises from believing in separateness whereas these not so small Divine moments of owning a silly nickname, moving from home, and building confidence with a broken-down horse exemplify the meaning of trust and vulnerability.

In reaching out to coworkers, a new family, or even a horse, I opened myself up to the possibility of healing, to the understanding that to experience love and connection, vulnerability is demanded.

Vulnerability, openness, transparency, all words to describe the action of trust. And trust is the precursor to love and healing.

Suffering is also isolating but can be transformed into hope through recognizing the things that truly bind us all.

Chapter 2

From Suffering to Hope

Something we were withholding made us weak,
Until we found it was ourselves.
-   Robert Frost
The Gift Outright

What's wrong with you?

I hear that question from strangers even today and it still makes my heart stop for a moment; my lungs must be startled too because they forget to expand when this happens.

My initial response *could* be "why, nothing is wrong with me. Why do you ask?"

But I know what's coming next: "Why do you limp?" Or even, "My neighbor's daughter has cerebral palsy; do you know her?" And my personal favorite, "Don't you have one of those telethons?" (I'm not kidding).

Well, I usually just plaster a smile on my face, pretending to be the ambassador of cerebral palsy, and begin my spiel, "I was born with cerebral palsy; it's kind of like having a stroke in the womb, but just like with all kinds of strokes, it can be mild or severe. It's not contagious and it doesn't get progressively worse. So, I'm really quite lucky," (I'm betting that most people can tell I work in the medical profession with a statement like that).

Then, after providing my educational blurb, I inevitably hear, "Well, you do well for yourself, don't you?"

"Why, yes, thank you," I smile and think to myself, yes, thank you for poking and prodding at my sense of self. I now feel awkward, ugly, and ineffectual. I turn away, shut my eyes, and take a deep breath.

You do well for someone with cerebral palsy, I hear echoing in my head, knowing the standards for me are so, so much lower than anyone without cerebral palsy.

I must confess that there are days I wish someone did understand about the pain and overwhelming fatigue of spasticity. The pain I get when my body jumps from a loud noise, the fear of curbs because they don't have handrails, the excessive amount of concentration needed to walk and carry something at the same time, or walk and talk at the same time, the need to sit, then stand, then sit on one hip, then sit on the other hip, lean forward, lean back, it's tiring.

I'm conscious of my position *all the time*. Except when I fall, that is.

Rescue Mission

One of my dearest friends, a therapist co-worker, understood my distress with these kinds of questions from our patients.

Possibly due to his past experiences in combat while serving our country, or maybe just because he has a beautifully rotten, mischievous soul, he jumped into the conversation after one of our new patients asked about my limp.

"You haven't heard the story about Debra?" He asked our patient.

"No." Our patient shook his head.

"Well, she kinda wants to keep it a secret... she's modest about these things." My friend drawled, and I hid my smile. "She was in the Gulf War, you know."

"Really," our unsuspecting patient replied, wide-eyed.

"Well, I really shouldn't tell you all this but there was a secret mission."

"*Really*?" Our patient leaned in close to my friend as I stood off to the side.

"She got a medal for it you know." My friend whispered and nodded his head as our patient's eyes got bigger.

My friend held his finger to his lips, "Shhhh, nobody knows..."

Our patient nodded, and no one asked me about my limp after that.

Spaz

When I was a kid, I didn't know anyone with cerebral palsy and my folks didn't really talk about it. I wanted to learn more about myself, so I'd sneak into my parent's bedroom and read my mom's medical textbooks that were hidden in the bottom drawer of her nightstand.

Pictures in the text books showed school aged children with the eyes blocked out of the photos, presumably to hide their identities, even though they were naked. When I saw those pictures of naked children with varying degrees of deformity, a twisted leg here, a raised shoulder there, I studied them closely, trying to reach through the pages. I was longing to touch them, to feel their arms and their legs that looked like mine.

It was so quiet, so hushed, and the earth stood still as I studied those photographs. I felt a strange mixture of longing, guilt, shame, and fear that I would somehow find my own picture in one of those books.

These medical texts coldly explained that cerebral palsy is a birth defect; that I was defective but also that there was no way to fix me; all the medical establishment could do for me was to photograph me and put me in a medical textbook for students' curiosity.

Due to my spasticity, medications such as muscle relaxants were prescribed frequently in my childhood, adolescence, and early adulthood; bedrest was often prescribed for a week at a time. I missed 20-30 days of school each year due to spasticity and subsequent pain.

Bedrest and muscle relaxers are a great way to create a socially isolated, emotionally depressed, and physically weak child but it did numb the pain.

Or it just numbed me. I had been on this regimen of muscle relaxers and bedrest from about age four or five through my mid-twenties when I decided that I didn't want to have pills around me anymore.

It was all too easy to keep myself drugged and pain free; I knew this was a path to self-destruction, but I would need to learn this through pain and not wisdom.

I did find that in working with my patients, I had developed a sensitivity to their physical and psychological pain that may not have been present had I not been living with pain myself.

My patient's and I used non-medication techniques to manage pain and spasticity while engaging in our everyday activities; we checked in with each other throughout our days and developed bonds of shared experience.

This seemed to give pain meaning for me; it was a profound mind shift, from ending my pain to finding a purpose in my pain. No longer would I focus on pain; I would focus on meaning. And the meaning for me was about caring for others, connecting to others, trusting in rightness of each and every days' experiences.

Purple Butterflies

Even though I hadn't worn leg braces since I was ten years old, I was still taking spills and picking myself up again. I still felt the old sad resignation, a stone in my chest, but I tried to hide my difficulties from others. I was still extremely self-conscious even though I tried to laugh and joke at my own clumsiness if others were around.

Despite trying to make light of my falls, it was becoming considerably more dangerous for me, in light of my newly diagnosed osteoporosis.

As I've aged, I've become susceptible to breaking bones during a fall; I wasn't worried so much about breaking bone as much as I was frightened of surgery to fix those bones. I've got a healthy fear of going under the knife, but it took several more falls and an injury to convince myself, finally, that I needed the support of leg braces

I worked with a quiet unassuming orthotist who wore leg braces due to a bout with polio; I was overjoyed! I was overjoyed not that he had a bout with polio, of course, but rather that here was a man who lived my life, a life of falling often, crawling on the floor occasionally, but with the need to take care of himself.

Here was the man who would design my braces. Due to advances in technology, I could wear a type of brace made of hard plastic with soft Velcro straps. This wouldn't be fun, but it was not a prison like the metal braces of my childhood had been.

I was breathing a bit easier and was feeling more comfortable especially since I could talk freely with my orthotist. His calming and pragmatic attitude gave me courage to ask if I could have the braces molded for regular shoes, not orthopedic shoes.

I wanted to feel somewhat feminine. I didn't want to let go of my new sense of femininity and sensuality. I was a newlywed! I didn't want to be reminded of my aging but rather my sense of style and beauty.

I could even incorporate a pattern on my braces instead of wearing the traditional institutional white. There were American flags, camouflage, Harley Davidson, Hello Kitty, but none of those seemed right. I wanted something else, then I saw it. I saw the pattern that would reflect transformation, beauty, fun, and life - purple butterflies!

Purple butterflies would be my totem, my spirit animals as in Native American culture, to remind me of change and transformation, to remind me of being unfettered by gravity, with shame being my "gravity." These butterflies would also symbolize my freedom from shame.

I would be visible; I would be proud to wear my purple butterflies, like a war paint or tattoo. I would continue to defy shame and suffering, grinding them into the ground with every step.

Winds of Change

In August of 1992 I was living in South Florida and working in a small transitional living center, housed in a five-bedroom house, with an enclosed front porch (serving as office space), a large open kitchen, a living room, and also an enclosed back patio (serving as a gym space). It served folks who suffered traumatic brain injuries as adults, from car accidents, motor cycle and bike accidents, gunshot wounds, suicide attempts, axe wounds, and from suffocation.

It was such a lively and energetic place; our patients worked on cooking, grocery shopping, doing laundry, crossing the street, you name it, we did it. We were proud that our patients were going to be able to go home, knowing how to care for themselves, after such horrific tragedies in their lives.

The work crew was close; we were a family and the work itself was fun and meaningful. But we had a Hurricane named Andrew coming and our home was in the evacuation area. We had only a few patients, including a quadriplegic patient, but a lot of us staff lived in the evacuation zone, so we packed up quickly and took ourselves to a designated medical shelter.

We knew we'd be back to work in a day or so; we decided to make it fun as we settled in on the second-floor gym of the local community college.

The college was a big, ugly, square, concrete structure, but this was to be our home for the next twelve to twenty-four hours; we brought games and music for ourselves as well as for our patients, knowing it would probably be a long and boring night.

Groups of medical professionals and patients from other facilities who were in the evacuation zone slowly trickled into the shelter as Hurricane Andrew was expected to make landfall. One charitable group had wisely brought food and made giant pots of spaghetti; everyone in the shelter was able to have a hot meal. There was the sound of laughter and chatting mixed with music, the smell of spaghetti, and the bright lights of an adult slumber party. Our patients were doing well, and we were stretched out on the floor, enjoying this new adventure.

I had asked my mom to meet us at the shelter even though she was not in the evacuation zone. I was worried about her, I knew she had been receiving treatment at home for a leg wound that just wouldn't heal.

She would need to stay off the leg for quite a few more weeks, or she'd run the risk of actually losing her leg. As a diabetic, my mom understood the gravity of the situation; she was terrified of losing her leg. We felt she would be safer in a medical shelter, with immediate access to healthcare professionals.

My uncle brought her to the shelter in a borrowed wheel chair and she brought a suitcase with her. Her leg was well-bandaged, and she didn't complain of any pain; I was glad mom was there with me and that she was safe. So, mom and I hung out together and we played scrabble while lying on floor mats to wait out the storm.

We heard wind gusting, and then the power went out. The giggling of anxiety filled the room then battery powered lanterns were turned on. The conversations continued although softer as if the power going out had turned the room's volume knob down.

Then I saw something pink floating in the air; this was confusing, I couldn't figure out what I was looking at. I saw clouds of pink dust in front of me. I looked up and noticed the ceiling was disintegrating.

A sudden thought popped into my head; I needed to get under something before the ceiling fell on my head. I was as paralyzed as our quadriplegic patient. Patients, staff, my mom and I were then swept up in the maelstrom of hysteria as we were forced under the wooden bleachers along the side wall.

I held my mother's hand; she wasn't in her wheelchair. The wheelchair was lost somewhere in the tide of people rushing toward the bleachers.

Then suddenly a hole appeared where a wall had

been; the storm, a freight train, was now inside the shelter. Larger and larger pieces of the ceiling were swirling in the room, then hitting the floor.

Mom and I were looking at pandemonium from under the bleachers that would soon become matchsticks. We held hands and turned to face each other. We found rubbery smiles on our faces, each trying to be strong for the other.

"Well, this might be it; I love you mom." I croaked.

"I love you, too." she said softly.

It's true that tall men are leaders, our boss was the tallest man in the shelter and he presently gathered all of us around him. He explained that our shelter was now compromised and that we must quickly move downstairs below the gym into the safer locker room areas.

This shelter had external stairs.

Although concrete, these stairs were open to the elements. We would be moving down a concrete stairway in a hurricane. And we had a quadriplegic patient, in his wheelchair, to move down a flight of stairs in the midst of at least 150 mph winds. Not a problem.

With fear driving our hurried movements, our patients were carried in their wheelchairs or in arms down this full flight of steps, sheltered by staff crowded on all sides of them acting as wind breaks. My mother was brought down also so she wouldn't be forced to put weight on her legs, her wheelchair was not to be found.

After reaching the stairway landing, we quickly discovered the barrier of sand bags about two feet high, blocking our way into the locker rooms. People in front of me and people behind me carried me up and over these bags and into two feet of water. This water was filthy, filled with bits of trees, soil, building materials and human waste. Only the lights powered by dimming batteries could guide our way.

We crawled over each other, and over mysterious objects floating in our way. We tripped and stumbled over things we couldn't see underwater.

I found my mom sitting on top of someone's luggage with her feet in the water; she had tried to lift her bandaged leg out of the water, but it seemed pointless. All of us were soaked after having braved the storm and now we were in the trash filled locker room ocean.

After having eaten and then evacuating downstairs to safety, it seemed everyone's bowels needed to evacuate as well.

The bathrooms in the locker room were horrific; the toilets were full to overflowing with people having been sick in the stalls. For the first but not only time, I let my bowels go and the terror of the past hour shot out of my bowels and into a plastic bag. There's really nothing like using a plastic bag as a toilet, I will just leave it at that.

It seemed hours went by, but the storm finally passed. Fearfully, we exited our locker room cave; went upstairs and in the light of day, we could acknowledge the miracle of our survival. There was a hole the size of a car in the concrete and rebar wall of our shelter. And there was a lonely wheelchair amongst the mountain of trash in the room.

Outside was a desert, a wasteland. Where were the trees? Where did the grass go? Is that the road, really? Where are the signs, the traffic lights? I know I live across the street from the shelter but where is my house? Am I looking east or west? Where do I live? Did the building get turned around? I know I live in that direction, don't I?

Well these questions couldn't be answered now, we needed shelter for our patients and for ourselves; we packed ourselves into cars and attempted to find safe haven at a staff member's house. There were four patients and about fifteen of us staff.

My mom's wheel chair had been found in the debris and she was able to keep her suitcase with her. After a car ride to a co-worker's home, mom got my dazed attention, "The daylight is going; you need to take care of my leg before it gets dark."

I was startled out of my daydream, replaying the worst moments of the storm in my head. As she said this, I heard an unspoken apology and I realized this was something she was unable to do for herself and she would spare me this if she could.

She let me push her wheelchair outside where we had good light; she had her suitcase in her lap.

She instructed me to lay the suitcase down and open the zipper; inside the case were bandages, 2 x 2 gauze, 4 x 4 gauze, Kling dressings, Kerlix bandage rolls, petroleum products, Chux pads, as well as scissors and forceps that had been sterilized and put in a plastic bag.

I also saw the insulin that needed to be refrigerated; we both looked at the insulin and said nothing. We wouldn't have refrigeration for over a month. I'd seen what a diabetic coma looks like; I'd seen what hyperglycemia looks like too. We both knew.

Mom had packed this suitcase as if her life depended on it and now her life *did* depend on it.

I laid a barrier down on the sidewalk and stupidly said, "This isn't sterile." and mom just replied, "Nothing is sterile now."

The unraveling of the old bandages began; as my mother began to softly instruct me to remove the first, then second, then third and fourth layers, I knew each tug, pull, touch, tap, bump, was agony to her but she was stoic. My breathing was shallow, and my fingers were numb. After all the bandages were off, I realized my face was wet; I was crying.

Christ, I thought, *my tears aren't sterile, I can't be crying now.*

There was a spot about as big as a Kennedy half dollar on her leg. It had a little gauze tapped in it; mom told me to just use the forceps to get it out. I tugged, a bit lifted off her leg, so I tugged more, and then a little more lifted, I tugged again. This was beginning to look like a long white ribbon,

Oh my God, I prayed. *Oh my God,* I thought, the words just kept running together in my head *OhmyGawd, omaGahdddd, noooooo.* I was holding my breath; my teeth were clenched.

I pulled out a yard of dressing; I was scared to look at her leg, but I didn't smell anything. *That's surely a good sign if it doesn't smell,* I told myself.

But then I looked. I looked at that little, innocent, gray hole inside her leg. *I don't think it's supposed to be gray, maybe her medicine for her leg is gray, or maybe it turns gray, or maybe gray is good,* my thoughts were tumbling over themselves.

My mom and I just kept quiet and we began the process of cleaning her wound, then re-bandaging it. By now my tears were flowing freely but my mom and I were quiet; we did our job then threw away the trash.

One of my coworkers was able to drop me off a little less than a mile from my townhome the next day; I walked and fell around debris, including downed trees, then I waded and fell in water, and then I fell in to my home. The floors and kitchen cabinets were wet, and my ceiling was wet, but I had four walls and a roof.

I had no power and no water, but I had a gas stove; none of us had power for over a month. Now August in South Florida is about as miserable as can be imagined, but without running water, and with the smell of mold growing in the house, it felt like I was in my own wet coffin.

My body and my mind were in a kind of fever; I think the city was in a fever.

No one knew who was where. No one knew how to get out of their homes. No one knew how to get to their jobs.

Days later, when an ambulance could drive through the chaos of downed power lines and trees, my mom was taken to the hospital because of the wound; this was a mixed blessing for her since the hospital had electricity, healthy food, and a comfortable bed for her to be in.

I went to see if her apartment was still standing. Her apartment building looked like a doll's house with one outer wall missing; it looked as if some giant child had been playing, got angry at her toys, and just smashed the dollhouse to the ground.

Mom never got to see her home again. Not only might she have to suffer the loss of her home but her leg as well. Masking my dread, I went to see her while she was in the hospital. She and I held each other close and I stroked her hair and rubbed her back; I rocked her and murmured nonsensical words. I massaged her legs and told her that I loved her. She was my child to comfort.

After a month, mom left the hospital; she had not lost her leg and she was well enough to go home. Since she had no home and she was unable to manage the stairs at my home, she decided to live with a friend from her church, even though they still had no power. I was glad mom had friends to care for her because I had only just started back at work.

Her friends called me one day to say that mom hadn't woken up that morning and was currently in the Intensive Care Unit at the hospital she had recently been discharged from.

I yelled, screamed, and stomped around the house until my throat was sore; then I went to the ICU. She was on a ventilator, I spoke to her and massaged her arms and legs a bit even though she didn't respond to my voice or my touch. I was stone; I was cold. I couldn't see, hear, or feel. Nothing could touch me.

Then I drove an hour out of town, met with friends, ate, then promptly vomited.

The next day, I asked the doctors for test results; those scans revealed that her brain was essentially drowning in blood. She had no brain activity but was being kept alive while on a ventilator.

I felt like a hollow tube as I called her friends, her church, and a local funeral home. Life was like water just running through me and nothing would stick.

I was an actor; I was a fraud. I wasn't able to go on anymore. I just wanted everything to stop so I could catch my breath.

I pretended that I was alive inside as I arranged a time for me and mom to be together as the life support was discontinued; I saw a tear fall out of her left eye and I knew I couldn't give her life back to her.

I told her she was free now.

Initially I told myself she had died when she had her stroke; I told myself it was what she wanted but my chest felt tight all the time. I felt guilty and I questioned my decision. My thoughts were spinning like a tornado in my head.

The quiet came once I acknowledged that she was alive while on life support and that she was dead after I decided to remove the life support. It was a stunning realization, like being hit with a hammer, that I made the decision to end her life. Was it a wrong choice? I don't believe that it was wrong but how could it be right if I ended her life?

If I was wrong to do it, then I still believe I was kind to do it. And I would not do anything different if faced with that dilemma again. It is still a burden to carry although I carry this burden out of love for her.

Giving love, giving care, and giving of oneself, lead

the way through suffering, to the destination of hope. By reaching out to others, pain and sorrow are given powerful and life changing meaning.

Hope is the butterfly from pupae, the apple from seed, the man from embryo, and the star from atom. Hope, life force, prime mover, alpha and omega, God - these are the words to describe the Divine in action.

Chapter 3

From Self Destruction to Self-Love

*That which we do not bring to consciousness
appears in our lives as fate.*
- C.G. Jung

First Love

One of the first people I met at university was to become one of the most significant people in my life. He became my first boyfriend ever, my first innocent and overwhelming love, and later my first committed long-term relationship. We studied together, danced together, explored new venues together, and we explored ourselves as well as each other.

I remember meeting him the first day of school, being struck by his curly blonde hair, his big smile and his gymnast's body; what could he see in an awkward, shy, preppy girl with glasses and a limp? I certainly couldn't do gymnastics or walk on my hands, but he loved entertaining me with tumbling, jumping and climbing feats. He made me laugh and smile; I was happy.

 Our first date was at a restaurant where we sat on the floor! I initially panicked but thank goodness we were seated next to a railing, so I could pull myself up at the end of the evening! Sitting on the floor in a public place was new and fun. I watched other couples with wine, leaning close to each other. Soft string music was playing. There was an intimacy in sitting on the floor that I never had when seated across from someone while in a chair. It was reminiscent of childhood games played on the ground or floor.

My boyfriend introduced me to sushi, to dating, to kissing, and then to love. He enjoyed my body, and this made me love him all the more. Here was a smart, beautiful man who not only enjoyed my company, he enjoyed studying with me and he loved loving me!

Since we both lived at home, our trysts were fun and unique; we made love in a meadow once, the breeze and the sunshine making love to my body just as he did. We were monogamous but, after two years, he wasn't able to contain his energy and love for just me; he had other women in his life he wished to love also.

I couldn't understand his need for other women in his life and I was extremely hurt and jealous. I believed that true love meant monogamy; he was wrong to have sex with or love more than one person at a time. When we separated, I was lost in the desert, confused, insecure, and unsure of myself. But in rejecting him and his lifestyle, I found myself taking on those same behaviors I had criticized in him as being unnatural.

Two Bunks and a Drunk

I had relationships, actually many mind-numbing, soul obliterating experiences, with different men and with women as well.

I tried to find love, diversion, pleasure, oblivion, forgiveness, stimulation, healing and connection. I found broken bits and pieces of what I was looking for, but none fulfilling. Nothing could fill that hungry, yawing mouth of depression.

In addition to the many encounters, or because of them, I was drinking heavily and frequenting nightclubs several times a week. I drank to quiet the clamor of my self-destructive thoughts.

Even when the drinking was out of control, I consoled myself with being a *regular*, with a sense of belonging afforded to those of us known as bar flies.

I often waited until the bars closed, about four in the morning, until I would get in my car and head home.

It was a small surprise to find myself in jail.

After striking a palm tree, while doing forty MPH in a twenty MPH zone, I looked up to see flashing lights. My glasses had flown off my head during the impact, but I easily recognized the blue flashing lights. I was bewildered, wondering how the cops had gotten to me so quickly.

It may have been when I had pulled over on the side of the road, opened the driver's side door, and vomited in the road, about a mile before said palm tree.

I had a suspicion that they were following me.

Of course, since I was driving home after drinking at a nightclub, I was wearing my tough girl combat boots, black eyeliner running down my face, and a fetching schoolgirl uniform. I wondered why the officer was just looking at me and shaking his head; I think he smiled or maybe it was a grimace.

Jail, in The Big City, on a Saturday night, consisted of me, a self-proclaimed prostitute, a woman wearing a muumuu (and nothing else) in for grand theft auto, and another drunk like me but who wanted to get home to her 5 kids.

I was quiet and sat on the floor, listening to how roughly the cops had treated my new best friend the prostitute during her arrest. Her wrists were chafed from when they had roughly pushed her into the back seat of the cop car.

I listened to how muumuu lady had cleverly stolen a car but still ended up in jail; I wondered if she hid the car in her muumuu. And was there any way to turn down the brightness of her orange and yellow garment? My eyes and head were beginning to hurt.

And the other drunk woman couldn't stop crying; apparently, she couldn't hold her liquor either, but I didn't say this out loud.

I had to pee, but the toilet was in the center of the

room; the chafed prostitute was using the toilet as a chair. I imagined that asking her to move, so I could pee, might endanger the tenuous bonds of our friendship.

Eventually, a large woman, who took up the entire space of the jail doorframe and wearing brown polyester pants with a button-popping, shield-bearing brown shirt, and with a sweet southern accent opened the door. She led each woman out the door, one at time, first the prostitute, then grand theft auto lady, and then the drunk with five kids. I was the only one left in the room, waiting to be strip searched.

Soon it was my turn; I heard her say in her sweet-as-molasses voice, in her warm timbre, "Honey child, what choo doin' here?"

It was then I began to cry, actually I began to bawl and hiccup, "I-I-I," I hiccuped. "I don't," I hiccuped again. "Kn, kn, knowwwwwwww." I wailed.

She just slowly shook her head, said she didn't need to search me, and put me in a room with two bunks and a drunk.

My luck was changing, and I was not so drunk after all; I wiped my eyes and nose.

I had believed that I was sobering up, but I had one more crucial decision to make. Who would I contact for my one and only phone call? Obviously, I was still intoxicated because I called.... my mother.

Luckily right beside the phone was the name and location of the jail; this was essentially a *what to say to the person who is going to bail your sorry ass out of jail...* list.

My mother arrived. Thankfully, my uncle was driving and smirking; he asked if I needed a runny-egg breakfast. He tried making this an adventure, but mom was self-absorbed.

My mother was sobbing and moaning (clutching at her heart), "I didn't even know you drank," which to me, even in my inebriated state, sounded hollow and false because I kept my wine in our common refrigerator and my Amaretto in our cupboard at home. Oh well.

Later that day, my father, the man I hadn't seen or spoken to in months, came to the rescue. He came over to the apartment where my mom and I were living after their recent divorce and he helped me get my $300, primer painted, repo car out of the impound lot and asked me in a gentle voice *why the hell I called my mom and not him.*

I was not surprised but actually shocked. I had expected harsh words and anger from him. I had expected disappointment and disgust. Instead, he told me about his own mistakes growing up, including a serious motorcycle accident, after a night of binge drinking.

I was touched at how he wanted me to call him if I were ever in trouble. I told him the truth, I didn't know why I hadn't called him, and that hopefully I wouldn't need this help ever again. I felt a softening toward my dad firstly that he would help me, and secondly, he didn't want to worry my mom.

He wasn't all tough and mean but rather more like a fire extinguisher, unseen and in the background, but there in an emergency.

I had come to realize that my father cared for me. He loved me.

Spending a night in jail was a harsh lesson but I can see it as an obvious turning point in my life; I was fooling myself if I thought my drinking was just for fun. And being intoxicated did not actually numb those hurt feelings inside me. I didn't want to hurt anymore; I wanted to reach out to others, but I wasn't yet able to open myself up to love.

One self-destructive behavior down but more to go.

Room 304

I hated myself for my inability to have relationships, but I kept reaching out to others for that physical and sexual connection. I believed that a physical or sexual connection was all that I was worthy of having. I told myself that a soul and spiritual connection was just for romance novels and love songs, not for real people.

At one point, I was having encounters with men I had just met online. I was reckless. I was foolish and self-destructive. After one potentially dangerous encounter with a young, well dressed, and rich stranger, I grew frightened as well.

I'd met who I thought was a well-educated, wealthy, interesting man who had been looking for companionship while living at an exclusive Miami Beach boutique hotel, at least that's what I saw online.

I dressed in a somber three-piece suit with a trendy coat and set out to find this tiny boutique hotel on the beach. I was nervous, and nauseous at the same time, but I still had this crazy thought that if this man was wealthy and into the Miami scene, he might also be so enamored of me that he would fall in love with me and take care of me for the rest of my life. I don't know why I let this thought draw me into reckless assignations.

I thought that I was doing all the right things by wearing the right clothes, listening to the right music, discussing the right books, and stepping into the lifestyle; I wasn't wealthy, but I could pretend to be part of the jet set.

I kept telling myself as I drove down the expressway, found the parking lot and even as I was walking toward his room, that I should just turn around. No harm done. I felt like I was in a dream, not my own dream but just some actor in a movie thriller. I kept silently yelling at myself to turn around, just like I'd yell at the character in a movie who was about to be killed in the first scene. But still my feet kept moving me forward. I saw a gray door, with 304 in gold.

He didn't answer the hotel room door; an unattractive, older woman with expensive clothes and a *two-hundred-dollar haircut*, answered the door but left as soon as I entered his room. Who was she, a body guard? A drug supplier? His girlfriend? His wife? Mom? I couldn't figure it out.

He was wearing the kind of torn and bleached out clothes that cost hundreds of dollars. I recognized them from Armani Exchange, this uniform was worn by many on the Miami Beach scene. He told me his shoes cost three hundred dollars and that he enjoyed designing shoes as a hobby. He then proudly showed me his closet filled with colorful and bizarre shoes.

He was slender, blonde, and looked much younger than I anticipated. He looked so unassuming and non-threatening.

I was prepared to have sex with him, that's what this was all about, wasn't it?! Going out for dinner and clubbing turned into room service in the hotel, which turned into pizza in the room which just turned into a soda in the room, which then became just sex.

He spoke of crazy violent things like putting hot curling irons or hangers inside me, but I still didn't leave. Why was he trying to scare me? Why did he smile as he said these things? Why was it so important to him that I needed to be intimidated?

He didn't attempt to touch me; I believed he wouldn't hurt me. I was blank faced and quiet.

We just got undressed and had sex in a rather plain hotel bed, in the missionary position, and he was done after about four minutes.

I tried to think of a reason to stay; he told me his *friend* was returning soon. I don't even remember speaking. I was numb; I was speechless. I felt nothing - not scared, or ashamed, or worried. I just got dressed and went home.

Why did I let this stranger have sex with me in a hotel room? I was sober and drug-free; there was nothing to impair my judgement. This was a suicide mission.

This was my attempt to remove myself from the earth, to stop pain, to stop all thought, to stop this madness, this unending cycle of self-disgust and self-destruction.

Gay Gary

When I was just 21 years old, who should drop into my life but a funny, sarcastic, intelligent artist; we spent the summer together, unemployed and free.

Later I discovered we had already met! Gary showed me where I had written in his junior high yearbook and wished him *all the best*. Seeing that yearbook entry gave our reunion that magic of fate or kismet.

It turned out that our meeting by chance on the metro rail would turn into one of the most significant moments of my life. He became my every day, every moment together friend; we were inseparable, and I would often stay with him at his parents' home on the weekends. He was gay and that afforded us a fun and playful relationship, as if he were a big brother.

I had sexual relationships with men, not friendships, up until this point. But now I discussed art, film, fashion, morality, and religion with him without the need to make him a boyfriend. Or at least that was my plan; I embarrassed us both by making a pass at him one night, but he graciously pretended it didn't happen when we awoke the next morning.

He didn't seem to notice my limp and he would often grab my hand if we were walking together. We would be walking down the Lincoln Road mall, and he would grab my hand and start running! I'd burst out laughing, trying to catch my breath, while trotting alongside, stumbling, and tripping but Gary never let me go.

After years of bright and stimulating friendship, we decided to rent an apartment together.

We had been roommates for several months when he told me he was HIV positive. I was struck by his matter of fact tone as I looked down at my hand at the glass of milk we had just shared. I had silly and panicked thoughts of becoming infected by sharing this glass of milk with him.

It was as if he had just put a match to the gasoline of my anger. I had such a tornado of feelings: fear, sadness, longing, and immense, over the top anger. I felt like my anger was huge, towering over me, and filling the room, suffocating me.

I made up reasons to not like him anymore, dirty dishes in the sink, using my laundry detergent, coming home late. I pretended those reasons were enough to end our friendship and not see him anymore after our lease was up.

My anger cooled, and sorrow took its place. I asked mutual friends how he was, and I was able to follow him for a year or so; then it seemed he disappeared. He and his family had moved to find better doctors, but no one had heard from him in months. I resigned myself to the certainty of his death; my heart was squeezed so small and I felt so hollow, as if in my chest was just an empty space.

Then, the phone rang late one night, a quiet and dreary night. It was Gary; he didn't say hi. He just started singing Elvis tunes.

"Wise men say, only fools rush in..." We sang, I laughed, I loved him, then he said goodbye.

He brought such joy in my life. My heart felt big, overflowing, and I felt full and loving. In opening my heart to receive his love, I discovered that the tight feeling in my heart was me holding tightly to love that must be given.

The hurt didn't come from lack of being loved but rather from not loving. Love needs to be given; that is the nature of love.

I used to think that love was that warm and fuzzy feeling I got when I was around puppies and newborn babies. I've learned that love is not about passively receiving feelings of closeness with nature or even oneness with the Divine. Those feelings come as a result of love but aren't actually what love is.

Love is much more powerful. Love requires that I become vulnerable, that I reach out to others. I don't believe that I have to love myself first before I can love someone else; I believe that I can only come to love myself by connecting to and caring for others.

Was this fate or had I somehow brought my jailor and my old friend into my life so that I could affect healing? In being given the opportunity to connect with people when I was at my lowest, most self-destructive self, I realized that even if I didn't love myself yet, maybe I could come to love myself if I found a way to love those friends, family, and yes, even strangers in my life.

Being generous implies having something to give; love is that thing I found inside myself not through solitude but through others around me.

While standing on the edge of the abyss, what do I hear but my soul crying out to connect with life, with nature, with art, with music, with others, and with myself.

Chapter 4

From Disgust to Empathy

*One thing that comes out in myths is that
at the bottom of the abyss comes the voice of
salvation.
The black moment is the moment when the
real message of transformation is going to come.
At the darkest moment comes the light.*

- Joseph Campbell (The Power of Myth)

In addition to the feelings of shame and suffering, I had distinct feelings of self-disgust related to my body and how I moved.

Winter Nightmare

I had a terrible recurring nightmare that played across the screen of my mind from childhood until my mid twenties.

I discovered myself dropped into a snow filled winter landscape, not a beautiful sparkling winter as in the Alps but rather a dirty, gray and bitterly cold Gulag type landscape. I was alone in this winter landscape filled with dark forests and an endless sea of snow-covered fields.

I was struggling mightily, trying to trudge through the snow that I sank into well above my knees. It was painful to breathe and move forward; I could feel the sharp cold air piercing my lungs. Around my waist, wound several times, and knotted, was a large rope, similar to the rope of a hangman's noose.

I turned my head and looked behind me to see only snow on the ground and the trees far off in the distance, indicating the many miles I had thus traveled. This rope, knotted, and digging into my waist fell behind me and was buried under the packed snow.

I twisted around; my legs were stuck in the snow, and I couldn't lift them up. I was able to pull the rope up and shake some of the snow off the rope; it was buried under the surface of my trail through the snow. I tried moving forward yet again. There was something at the other end of the rope, keeping me from moving forward.

A feeling of dread descended over me, like a cloak, suffocating me. My bowels were hollow; I couldn't, wouldn't look back. I began to weep angrily but I didn't look back again; I couldn't look back.

I just leaned forward, like a mule pulling an overly large workload, and slowly dragged this thing that was attached to me. I felt it getting snagged on rocks and branches and snow drifts, but I was too frightened to look back.

I kept fighting forward, crying and yelling out loud, waving my arms, trying to turn my fear into anger.

I'd take a deep breath, heart pounding, open my mouth to scream, then suddenly, I was awake.

This dream continued for several years until one night, I dared to look back to see what I was dragging. For years I had kept looking forward, trying to ignore what I was bringing with me. I dreaded looking back toward the end of that rope. I squeezed my eyes shut as I turned my head then I slowly opened my eyes.

It was a torso. A body without a head, without arms and without legs. I was dragging myself, a dead and featureless self, with terror, anger, and struggle.

After discovering what I was dragging in my dream, the nightmares stopped, and I could breathe again. With much sorrow and much mourning, I could let go of that featureless self and start breathing again.

I mourned those many years that I was too afraid to look back. I mourned for my twenty something year old self who had discovered a past filled with lightly disguised self-disgust.

I had feared my demons, my shadow side, my darkness; however, in the light of truth, I could mourn that part of myself. The dark side of me wasn't terrifying, it was simply hurting and suffering.

In the Confessional

Around the age of fourteen, I recognized feelings of disgust and shame related to the way I moved;

limping and swaying along. I would pull to the side and I leaned forward awkwardly as I moved.

I was sad, and I wanted this pain that was my life, to be over. I saw myself as impossibly ugly, disgustingly fat, horribly crippled, and totally useless. I couldn't see a way through this never-ending darkness; it was suffocating me.

I was in turmoil; my brain and my guts were in knots and I couldn't find peace from friends, from family, or from school. I believed the only option that was left was to see a priest. I had my doubts; what could a celibate man know of the overwhelming angst of a teenage girl? It was worth a try, so I made the arrangements.

Priests in the military wear uniforms when not celebrating mass, so it was not unusual to see a priest with combat boots and camouflage under his vestments. Those uniforms were reminders to me that these men are frail, fragile, and all too human; a priest isn't a priest all the time, only when he celebrates mass, or so I believed.

I was in a room with a dirty, banged up, gray metal desk with papers littered on it; there were two metal folding chairs and a broken metal bookcase. There were books sliding off the broken shelf. The floor was linoleum.

I couldn't look up to meet the eyes of the priest. This was no confessional but rather only an open room to meet with the priest face to face; I couldn't hide myself behind a black screen in a dark booth. There was no familiar scent of incense nor a padded kneeler. I would have to sit in a cold metal chair and talk about my shame in front of him.

The room was quiet, and it smelled like old... like metal and dust... not moldy but unused and makeshift. I thought this room might have been old storage.

The priest who was in one of the folding chairs was old too; he had white hair and a round belly. He had the foot of one leg resting on the knee of the other even though he was still in his vestments. He looked so incredibly old and bored; I couldn't speak to him. I just felt like I was shattering into a million pieces and couldn't be put back together again. There were tears forming.

I told him I was ugly and didn't want to live. He listened with his head tilted to the side. He tried to hold my gaze as I looked over his shoulder or down at the floor. His expression didn't change, except to maybe get a bit softer around the edges.

I was afraid to hear what he might tell me of my sins; I couldn't imagine a fitting punishment. Instead he gently told me to say a Hail Mary. But I wasn't to say a regular Hail Mary. This one would be different; I was to say my name instead of Mary:

> Hail Debbie
> Full of grace
> The Lord is with you

> Blessed art thou
> Among women
> And blessed is the fruit of thy womb,
> Jesus
> Holy Debbie
> Mother of god
> Pray for us sinners
> Now and at the hour
> Of our death... Amen
> (Luke 1:28, 1:42)

My mind hovered above myself. It swirled and danced. How could I be like the mother of god? How could I even consider myself holy?

How did this priest know to care for me, to let me know I am treasured? How did this priest know that I could be good?

I was shocked, startled, confused but I could see a glimmer of light where before I had seen only darkness. He showed me, with gentle wonder, how extraordinary I was, as important as the Mother of God, and that I was resting safely in the hands of God.

Suicide is a Four-Letter Word

Now I write about the part of myself that has yet to see the light of my vulnerability. It's an ugly part of me and it is an ugly truth as well. I would like to disguise this part of me and minimize the size of this monster that slinks to the surface of my consciousness.

During one trip to the doctor when I was about twelve or thirteen, after experiencing severe stomach pains for months, a heart murmur was discovered; but tests indicated that there was no real reason for the stomach aches that caused me to double over.

One of the doctors prescribed tranquilizers and antacid; I walked through the hallways in school swigging my bottle of Gelusil like it was a watery milkshake, white residue on my lips all day. The stomach aches continued.

The doctor actually called me at my home; my mom answered the call then stood by me as the doctor asked if there was anything I had wanted to tell him that I couldn't share earlier when I was at his office with my mom present.

I couldn't catch my breath; my mind went on the fritz as if it were hooked up to a stripped wire. I couldn't think of what to say.

I wanted to tell him about the crying jags, the arguments with my parents because of my crying, the anxiety about my mother's illness and probable death, the silence in the house that only I broke. My parents did not speak to each other; they spoke only to me.

I wanted to tell the Doctor I wanted to be pretty, and smart, and I didn't want to be a burden. I wanted to tell him my parents didn't have time for me and that

I needed to learn how to care for myself before they left me.

I was drowning in a dark ocean filled with riptides, towering waves, and unknown creatures but a quiet, self-assured, young doctor was throwing me a life line. He was so close, and I could feel my fingertips brushing against the life jacket; but I was frightened, and I let it slip away. There was something frightening about letting someone help me.

Because of my access to muscle relaxers and tranquilizers for my spasticity and my anxiety, it wasn't difficult to imagine overdosing as the ultimate and final escape. My first cry for help came at age thirteen. Crying jags seemed to be a part of my day, always after dinner with my parents continually asking, *what's wrong?* With confused looks on their faces. I just shook my head and cried.

Then, at sixteen, I spoke to my teacher about planning to commit suicide at school that day, also by overdosing on prescription medication.

At twenty-five, I ended up in the hospital after taking twenty muscle relaxer tablets and locking myself in my apartment; I believe my landlady was around to let the paramedics into the apartment that time.

I wasn't just in the planning stages of suicide; I had graduated to attempting suicide.

Although I sought psychiatric help in my twenties,

and received medications and talk therapy, the sadness and despair continued to affect how I lived from day to day. So, I threw away all my tranquilizers and muscle relaxers, and I tried to set up a suicide-free environment.

It wasn't until my late thirties that I met a social worker and physician who could work successfully with me. Or rather, we worked well together. We put a focus on finding the correct medications for my debilitating depression and my persistent anxiety while developing a way of recognizing and dealing with my intense bouts of darkness, and feelings of being in the dark hole.

At the age of forty-five, I signed myself into a psychiatric hospital day program; for two solid weeks, I participated in daily group therapy, individual therapy, and saw my doctor twice a day. I signed a document promising to not attempt suicide. How strange to promise a stranger that I would not attempt suicide; what if I broke my promise? Would I get in trouble?

I found myself wanting to fall into the healthcare provider role; I had to stop myself from leading group therapy. I wanted to delve into other people's issues rather than deal with my own. I definitely was more psychologically handicapped than physically handicapped at this point in my life; for some reason it was important that I not be blamed for being depressed.

All those feelings of shame resurfaced but not

because of a limp, but rather due to a flaw in my brain chemistry. I kept trying to figure out what I did wrong to be this way while my therapists were trying to show me that reaching out for help was not wrong but indeed *very sane.*

Seeing others, including a nurse, a cop, and a business man in group therapy, struggling with depression, turned my gaze outward from myself. In discovering the pain these people experienced and watching their determination to become vulnerable, I wanted to move forward in their footsteps. Healing happens with vulnerability and I wanted to be a part of the process.

The process of peeling those outer layers to reveal a newborn, soft and true self underneath was possible only by reaching out and building those connections with others. They were my new lifeline and I would grab it.

It Takes Two, Baby

One day, a colleague of mine came up to me while I was at my desk. She told me about these twin teenage girls, who had cerebral palsy, and how she had worked with them for many years. She had been their physical therapist and she suggested that I might like to provide much needed occupational therapy services to them.

At first, I sighed, took a deep breath, and tried to sound grateful even though I wanted to distance myself from being labeled, especially from being known as the cerebral palsy therapist.

I told her that I only treated adults, I had a full schedule, and that I probably couldn't even teach them anything about getting dressed or bathing themselves that they didn't already know.

My colleague was friendly but persistent and I figured that I could meet these girls, just so my colleague would stop bothering me about it. So, I agreed to just meet them and talk, more to satisfy my colleague than to actually treat them.

After the girls finished therapy with my colleague, they were brought into the office for our meeting. I was nervous and trying to figure out what to say to these strangers, twin teenage girls specifically.

I imagined the comic and awkward:

> *So, I see you have CP, well isn't that something.*

> *Gee, there are more people in this office with CP than those without it.*

> *You have done well for yourselves, haven't you?*

> *How's that new neurologist working for you?*

I needn't have concerned myself at all; these sisters were funny, gregarious, and curious about how I functioned. They wanted to know if I'd been called names or been patronized, or marginalized. They wanted to know how I lived with spasticity and pain, if I fell and how I got back up.

The hours flew and the people around us seemed to fade away. I had never before been able to communicate with any certainty, the degree and type of pain I experienced, how liberating to speak and to be understood.

Not only did I feel understood, I had the ability to understand. I knew what having CP was all about; I knew what it was like to be an adolescent. I certainly couldn't know everything about these young women, but I could try. I discovered that I wanted to try.

I had stopped talking about my difficulties because I believed they could not be understood by the people in my life; sharing my difficulties had seemed self-centered, and unimportant. When these twins stepped (wheeled?) into my life, I realized that in keeping quiet about my problems, I had also buried a significant part of myself.

We worked together on all those things that are so important to a teenage girl.

How do I cut my steak when I go out to dinner on my first date if I can only use one hand?

How do I do my hair so that my mom doesn't have to do it anymore?

How do I manage the buttons on my button-down shirt that makes me look so good?

How do I put on earrings?

How can I help mom when she does so much for me?

Can I wear lace up shoes?

Can I tie a bow?

What about getting a soda out of the vending machine at school?

Am I pretty?

And how do I grow up?

Who is my role model?

Will I be able to live on my own?

What about college?

Who understands me? My frustration? My pain? My needs?

How do I tell people what I need if I'm not sure myself?

We talked about how people do judge us by our appearance, and we spoke of the awkwardness of being in a wheelchair. We talked about fashion and fitting in to the mainstream, wanting to be popular. Even though my girls didn't move like other girls in their classes at school, they were still teenage girls.

Meeting these young girls was an opportunity for me to revisit my own teen years. I saw in them a certainty, a wholeness, a sense of self, and a hopefulness that I longed for in my own life.

Through sharing and connecting with them, being vulnerable, I was able to rediscover my unique purpose, my reason for being. I found a reason for being, not a reason for doing necessarily, but a worthiness in just being who I am.

They taught me through their words and actions; they had hope for their future, certainty in their beauty, faith in their purpose, and courage in reaching out to others.

They taught me self-love.

Chapter 5

From Fear to Courage

To let go means to give up coercing, resisting, or struggling, in exchange for something more powerful and wholesome which comes out of allowing things to be as they are....

Jon Kabat-Zinn
(Wherever You Go There You Are)

A lifetime of fear and anxiety could not be dismissed easily by my self-destructive behaviors; I needed to find another way to cope. My coping strategy wasn't really a strategy at all; I just tried to let everything go, to fly out of my overburdened mind.

My Achilles Heel

Without my leg braces forcing my feet down and keeping my legs straight, I began to move about on my tiptoes and with my feet turned inward. Although I lurched and swayed and leaned precariously forward, this was MY normal. It was easy, and I didn't have to concentrate to move around. Sure, I fell a lot, but I just got up and kept going.

I was anxiously and excitedly waiting for the day I could get surgery to make me walk like everyone else. My family and my doctors told me that when my bones were long enough and when I was tall enough, I would get my surgery! This was going to be my magic surgery!

I would walk and hold my head up; I wouldn't have to look down at my feet all the time to prevent myself from tripping. I would carry my schoolbooks and walk at the same time without stumbling. I would run, and I would ride a bike. Or roller skate. Or play kickball.

I would look right in my clothes. My pants wouldn't bunch up on one side or get twisted around my waist. I would be just like everyone else. I would belong.

I held onto those promises with fierce determination.

I longed for this miracle surgery; each year I wanted to know if this would be the year. I would hold my breath, cross my fingers, and try to keep from squirming as I waited on the exam table each year, hopeful that this would be the magic year. The year I turned twelve was my lucky year.

I felt so grown up when my mom and I met the surgeon; I was a bit queasy and nervous, imagining that he would open me up and perform the surgery in his office. But I could handle anything because I would soon walk normally. My doctor's name was Dr. Nutt. My mom made a joke about his name, but I thought making a joke about his name was awfully bad luck.

I was so excited for surgery, I remember being on the operating table, counting down from 100, I believe I made it to 99. I knew the surgeon would fix me.

When I woke up, I saw my family near me and I was so excited to get up out of bed to experience walking normally. I was hurt and surprised when they told me I had to stay in bed. A physical therapist would walk with me later the next day.

My mom helped me put on my bathrobe that had pink polka dots and lace; this was the special robe my mom had made me for my surgery. I was excited to be getting up and walking. Maybe I could try running too.

Since I had my surgery in a military hospital, my physical therapist was a navy officer. He had curly dark hair, and a big smile. We locked eyes; he was oh so handsome and everyone else in the room seemed to disappear. I was at one end of the parallel bars in a wheelchair with my fully casted right leg resting in front of me and he said,

"Walk for me, Debbie."

I'm certain I heard church bells ring and the flutter of angels' wings. I don't know whether it was hypotension or love, but I swooned.

I was light headed and smiling. I must have pulled myself up and walked, because I was moving toward his open arms. I had found my heart's desire, my reason for living, and an analgesic. Love is a great pain reliever; I didn't feel even a twinge of discomfort during our therapy sessions over the next week or so.

Time seemed to fly by swiftly while I was in the hospital and soon, I would be going home. Once home, I could get back into my routine, take care of myself, and get back to school with the added burden of a fully casted leg.

The weight of my full leg cast made it feel like I was dragging a concrete block; I needed a walker to hold onto so that I could lift myself and swing my legs through. It was extremely tiring, and my classmates called me *crippled* and *gimp* when they saw me in the hallways moving from class to class. Even though I was angry and ashamed, I knew I would soon be walking like everyone else.

After many long weeks of waiting, the big day finally was here; I would get my cast off! My parents seemed almost as excited as I was; we waited for the grinding of the cast saw to stop.

I was not prepared for the sight and smell of my casted leg; we brushed the dead skin off my leg, it had such a pungent sour smell. I wrinkled my nose, but I still wanted to see my new leg. I was confused; it looked so pale and skinny. It didn't feel connected to me; I couldn't make it move. I picked my leg up with both hands; it was heavy as I swung it over the exam table.

Even though I was confused, I held onto the belief that once I put my foot on the floor, it would know how to make me walk normally. But I still needed something to hold onto as I walked; I was uncertain and unsteady on my feet and they didn't feel totally connected to my body yet. I needed to watch my feet to make sure they went where I wanted them to go. A not so little voice inside my head was getting concerned about my being so wobbly and about my needing to use a walker for stability.

My self-confidence and my certainty about being normal was quickly eroding, like a monstrous landslide, carrying then suffocating all life before it. My body seemed to be floating, and my mind disconnected. I had placed not only my faith but my entire sense of self, of worthiness, in a simple surgery.

I cried hard and didn't know what to do; I just couldn't lift my leg without falling down. I could feel the blood rush to my face and head; I felt hot, angry, and ashamed. I couldn't look my dad in the face; I just kept my head down, watching my feet and willing them to move.

After an eternity, my dad helped me out of the hospital, to the car, and home.

Hanging Around

Early in my career, I was part of a fun and exciting team building exercise course called Ropes, in which about forty staff members participated in an outdoor picnic activity day filled with challenges to our ability to trust and work with others.

We had blind trust walks in which one person would lead another person who was blind folded through an uneven and unknown path from danger to safety.

Another activity involved the trust of a person on a platform falling backward into a crowd of waiting arms.

The final activity involved each member individually climbing a modified telephone pole and crossing a single rope bridge while being held by rope to those team members on the ground entrusted to ensure each climber's safety.

I remember being on the ground and watching each climber get ready with a safety helmet and ropes with carabiners, big nervous smiles on the climbers' faces. Then I watched as each climber approached the pole and slowly climbed, getting smaller and much further away from the ground within moments. Each step was made slowly and carefully, using sturdy hand and footholds, the folks on the ground were cheering.

I saw each climber stretch from the final step and reach for the rope hand and foot holds. Both ropes bounced as each person attempted to stand on one rope while using another rope to pull oneself up tall. Each person would jack knife at the hips and would move to a sitting position, often yanking on the rope in hand to hoist themselves upright. Some people would hold themselves almost horizontally with feet in front of them and arms at their chest; they looked like they were in an invisible bed.

When someone lost their footing or hand hold, the folks on the ground would hold their own ropes steady, slowly lowering the person from the air at the other end of their rope, to the safety of the ground.

I knew intellectually that this could be done; I didn't want to be the one who couldn't do what all my team mates *were capable of doing.* Was I more fearful of climbing or more fearful of my shame; certainly, my fear of heights could be dealt with; however, my shame would be never ending, like a stone embedded in my chest.

I placed my hands and feet on the pole, hugging the wood with my body, trying to attach myself to the pole with every movement. After much reaching and grunting, I came to the rope, using my left hand to reach out from the pole but still clinging to the pole with my right arm. I was too short, I couldn't reach the rope. But if I let go of the pole, I would be letting go of all I had to keep me safe. I was terrified; I couldn't do this. It wasn't possible.

But I surely couldn't back down, the people cheering me on didn't know I couldn't move my body to reach for the rope without falling.

I was going to fall. I felt hot tears start to form then,

I got so angry that I let go of the pole with my hands and I reached for the rope. I felt a tug at the ropes around my hips lifting me up, so I could step to the rope and get my footing. I made it! I was actually standing on a rope! I was holding myself up with the rope at chest height! I was sliding along and staying upright! Who knew ropes were easier to walk along than even ground?!

I don't remember the rest of the day, how I got home or even what company I was working for at the time; but being up in the sky moving along a rope, made me feel so connected to others, to nature, to my own body. I was comfortable in my body and was able to trust myself, trust others and trust the world around me. That trust liberated me from fear.

You Can't Do That!

I was about ten or so when I decided to become a ballerina; I loved watching them twirl and leap so beautifully. I watched their skirts float and gracefully skim their legs. I imagined my arms fluidly moving through the air, with delicate hands. I knew I would need lessons because that's what other girls in school did.

I performed my own version of leaps and twirls in the house while approaching my parents; I plopped in front of them and said, "I want to be a ballerina!"

I had a gigantic smile on my face and I was moving my arms as I spoke because I was so energetic. I would wear pink and I would have ballet shoes and I would be pretty.

"You can't do that."

And that's all it took to remove my smile, to take my enthusiasm, to dash my dream on jagged rocks. I became a small and crippled little girl.

Prima Ballerina

When I turned thirty, I decided that for this milestone birthday, I would take ballet lessons. My mom had died, and my father had moved away; no one could tell me that I couldn't take ballet lessons. I felt almost giddy as I began looking for ballet instructors.

As luck would have it, I found a dance school close to my home in the city; my teacher was almost ten years younger than me, but she was more than happy to give me lessons.

I had a nervous stomach as she put me at the barre; I was wearing leotards and a silky dance skirt. We listened to classical music and she drilled me in a variety of poses, standing at the mirror, performing exercises without a break. I left myself behind while entranced by classical music on the turntable.

We did this weekly with me wearing a ballerina smile during exhausting sessions at the barre. We attempted some poses and jumps away from the barre, in the middle of the floor dance space. This dance space was enormous, and I was frightened by not having something to hold onto for balance. My teacher was not concerned about my fear; all her students had fears.

I hopped about two inches from the floor. My ankles weren't flexible, and I landed as hard as a stack of books thrown on the floor. It was awkward; I was loud. It was difficult and no one except my teacher ever saw me or knew what I tried to do, but I was confident in myself. By being vulnerable, by stepping into my fears, I found a mentor as well as courage. I felt a surety, a solid, immovable part of my center that could not be denied or discouraged.

I was beautiful.

Sagrada Familia (the 400 steps)

For my friend's fiftieth birthday, three of us traveled to Madrid and Barcelona in Spain. I was enchanted by the beautiful architecture and cobblestone streets in Madrid; I was transported several centuries in time. There were no cars in the old city; it was a city for pedestrians. I saw both the hipster youth and the well-worn faces of the aged, robust and infirm, walking the city alleyways. I enjoyed seeing the elderly women walking arm in arm with the young; life was for both young and old.

I've had a joyous fascination with Gaudi and was eager to see the Sagrada Familia, the church of the Holy Family in Barcelona. It's filled with unusual images, arches, and organic shapes; the cathedral feels alive with movement. There are animals hidden in stone, the columns look like trees in a forest, and the stairs look like a nautilus.

After several hours waiting to enter the cathedral, we wandered about, with our jaws open and with shining eyes. I had goosebumps on my skin and felt as if I were in the presence of the Divine. There was a hush often found in art galleries and churches but there were also groups of men with chisels and hand tools repairing parts of the cathedral with the gentleness of true craftsmen. Workmen, worshippers and tourists mingled easily in this holy and wondrous place.

We waited for a tour guide to lead us up the elevator and show us the view from the windows through the spires of the cathedral. We could see the city of Barcelona spread out before us in a breath-taking panorama.

I was so caught up in the view and the magic of being in the sky that I got turned around and couldn't find the elevator. I was swept up in the crowds moving toward the stairwell. I vaguely recalled that the guide mentioned that the stairwell was only big enough for one person at a time, that once starting down, we couldn't stop or turn around. I remembered he told us there were no handrails in this narrow spiral.

The stairs were fashioned in a tightly twisted nautilus shape, but I hadn't realized where I was until I had been gently pushed forward by those behind me.

I began to panic although I could not resist by standing still; I was being moved forward step by step forever looking down but never able to see around a corner; there were no corners!

I felt alone but I heard angry voices above me in foreign languages. I knew people were angry with me for my lack of speed in descending these tightly wound stairs. I wanted to cry; I felt my face get hot. I wanted to yell that this was a beautiful and holy place. I wanted to stomp my feet and tell people to slow down, to let me breathe.

Anger and disgust sound the same in any language. Nobody wants me. Nobody likes me. I kept going. I found out later that it's about 400 steps. Wow.

My friends and I were reunited; we smiled and laughed when we found each other. I was relieved, but I didn't tell them about the people who were angry at me.

I'm proud I did 400 steps. But it is a long way down while listening to angry people.

North to Alaska

My friends planned on a seven-day cruise to Alaska from Vancouver when I was in my late twenties; I asked if I could tag along because, not only did I love to travel, I would see the majesty of glaciers.

Being on a cruise ship is a wonderfully easy way to travel; there are hand holds everywhere. My way of moving on land seems to be similar to how normal people walk while on a rocking boat. I was grateful for handrails in hallways and for rounded corners on furniture. I fell often, but onto soft couches and carpeted floors. I tried to don a formal gown while on stormy seas; I was held hostage by my pantyhose while rolling on the floor.

We had gourmet food and great fun on our trip. When it was finally time for my helicopter ride to a glacier; my friends were enjoying other excursions, so I was on my own this time. Initially our jaunt was cancelled due to poor weather on nearby glaciers however, an adventurous and outgoing pilot suggested we go to a glacier further away from port but with better weather.

I was so excited because I'd never been in a helicopter or on a glacier! According to my body weight, I was placed next to the pilot, squashed next to him with my knees pressed against a stick coming up from the floor console. I discovered that this stick controls where the helicopter goes after repositioning myself and accidentally hitting the stick with my knees. We began turning to the left, oops!

I had a grin plastered to my face and my hands were holding onto my seat in a death grip; my knuckles were bloodless from gripping so tightly. Part of the floor in the helicopter was plexiglass and I could see the magnificent ocean, barren land, and massive glaciers beneath my feet.

Finally, we landed, and the pilot helped each of us

out of the helicopter and on to the glacier; we were wearing special boots to help us stay upright while on the ice. I grabbed the pilot's hand and I moved about ten feet from the helicopter.

I quickly dropped to my hands and knees to keep my balance, pretending I was squatting to touch the ice and snow rather than lowering myself to keep from sliding on the ice.

The pilot took my picture as I was grinning and trying to maintain a squat. He and the others wandered off to explore. I looked around to make sure no one was near and crawled / swam my way back toward the helicopter, so I could pull myself upright to stand.

As I reached for a handhold on the helicopter to pull myself up, I felt the helicopter slide away from me! The helicopter was on skis on the glacier and I was pushing it toward a crevasse! Because the helicopter was moving away from me, it pulled me to stand and I promptly let go - dear God!

What if we are stranded on a glacier because some crazy woman who can't keep her balance accidentally pushed the helicopter into a crevasse going five miles down through the ice and permafrost!? What if we lost communications!? My heart hammered and almost escaped my chest.

Thankfully the pilot arrived with champagne and chocolate! He didn't seem to notice the skid marks under the helicopter, at least he didn't say anything.

I hoped that my red face just told him I was cold rather than ashamed and frightened.

I've decided that champagne and chocolate need to be in any survival kit I may carry in the future; it sure helped calm my nerves, so I could enjoy the otherworldliness of being on a glacier.

The color of blue is indescribable in its purity and vibrancy, almost a fantastical dreamy hue. This blue will always take my breath away and it will remind me of my adventures on MY glacier.

Would You Treat a Pedophile?

I worked at a hospital that had a unit set up to treat patients from the prison system, the Department of Corrections. As rehabilitation therapists, we didn't go on that unit although we did receive training from the DOC.

We knew to step aside if a police officer and a patient handcuffed to a gurney needed to enter or exit an elevator. We knew how to deliver CPR to someone handcuffed to a gurney. We were shown a variety of shivs made from everyday hospital supplies, so we knew to keep items out of reach of prisoners.

We all laughed and joked after our training, but I was still nervous about seeing prisoners in the hallways.

One day, our boss told us we would be treating a prisoner in our own department, not handcuffed and not escorted. We were told that he could not move and was not a threat.

He had apparently suffered his fifth stroke either from a beating in prison or as a result of high blood pressure. His MD recommended therapy to address his pain and to assess his potential ability to feed himself. He was a pedophile.

A pedophile. My brain just turned that word into slime, like the clog in a sink drain, filled with grease, hair, dirt, and trash. I imagined a man with red eyes and horns like a devil.

Our boss didn't know which therapist might treat him; our boss needed a volunteer. There were about twelve of us present; the room was silent. I looked around, then I said, "I guess I'll do it."

I Guess I'll Do it

I thought that because this was something I didn't want to do, then I MUST do it. Maybe it's the Roman Catholic upbringing but I just didn't want to be afraid when he was in the treatment gym. I thought that if I treated him, I might be able to control my fear of him.

He was brought into the treatment gym in a type of recliner; his arms and legs were like pretzels and his torso was twisted so that his hips faced to the side, but his head faced forward. He couldn't speak, and I don't know if he understood me.

I would have to touch him to teach him to hold a

spoon. I would have to place my hands over his. I tried not to think about what those hands had done. I wanted to be kind in the face of his depravity.

My conscience wouldn't let me refuse to help another person, no matter how distressed I was about it.

I treated him two or three times before he left; looking at his deformed body, I asked myself if I had sympathy for him. I was so terribly confused and conflicted. I found myself thinking that he deserved pain and suffering, but I was horrified to imagine that he might have been beaten regularly even while bed bound.

I don't think I could have good feelings for him, but I didn't want to hurt him or insult him. I didn't want to know him, but I could care about him, I think.

I'm glad I tried.

How do I possibly connect the experiences I had in my surgery and recovery, my desire to be a ballerina, my climbing a pole, my travel to a glacier, my descending a twisted stairwell, and my treatment of my patient?

These were about situations I either placed myself in or found myself in; some situations had happy endings, and some had not so happy endings.

These were such profound moments because of the intense emotions surrounding them. I felt such fear, confusion, doubt, and sometimes rage. I felt numb, dizzy, overwhelmed, and lost at times.

Was I courageous? Mostly, I just kept going. My feelings didn't resolve themselves and I didn't receive any epiphanies to bring me out of darkness. I just had to keep going, hoping that any direction was better than standing still.

There comes a time when the only control or power I have left is just to let go. Letting go of the result, letting go of the opinions of others, letting go of my feelings, all lead to a freedom and ease that comes from acceptance.

Acceptance is not about giving up but rather about giving over, about trust, about vulnerability.

And in that way, we find love.

Chapter 6

From Depression to Confidence and Purpose

Peace comes within the souls of men
when they realize their oneness with the universe.

-   Black Elk

To be able to give meaning to my sorrows allowed me to honor those travails and bring them to the light of truth. I was no longer concerned with hiding my sadness or pain; rather, I sought to use those experiences to strengthen my relationships with others.

You're Healed!

We had a new young priest come to the church to breathe life into the Church's traditional teachings. As mom grew more involved in her spiritual growth, I was swept along in this fast-moving river.

One evening, we were present at a large gathering in a town theatre, it had a well-lit stage and a podium with microphone where I knew something exciting was going to happen.

First there was singing with guitars and tambourines; people lifted their hands in the air and sang happy, uplifting music about love and joy.

I smiled as a looked around, but I felt a tiny bit of apprehension, like an ant crawling up my arm, not bothering or biting me but just letting me know it was there. I was younger than most people there; I must just not understand what was going on. This was church, kind of. Wasn't it?

The singing and clapping was fun; people were smiling, except for the people with their eyes closed and their hands raised. Their lips were moving, and they seemed to be whispering something, but I didn't understand, who were they were whispering to? They swayed and whispered; more and more people swayed, and the music tapered off.

 I heard voices from the crowd, but I didn't know what they were saying. It sounded Hindi or Arabic or Russian, something completely foreign, and people were speaking over each other, yelling out, not actually communicating.

Someone made their way to the stage while strange sounds came out of their mouth. I didn't understand how they could make it to the stage with their eyes closed and hands in the air. Soon others joined them on stage, trance-like and swaying. My breath caught in my throat; my chest was heavy, and my body hummed.

Someone yelled, "You're HEALED," on stage and voices grew louder, although I didn't know what those voices said.

People started toward the stage like a dripping

faucet being slowly turned to full blast. I found myself caught in that stream, being pushed to the stage, being lifted to the stage. I couldn't find mom.

I soon felt mom's hands on me, but they felt strange and unfamiliar; the stage was charged with energy. A circle formed around me as people prayed; I began to cry from fear, from hope, from sadness.

Then I was declared healed and carried away by several people. The rest of the night is a blur, but I felt so shamed from having needed to be healed.

I struggled with the inner voice that was beating on my brain, *what is so wrong with me that I need healing? Aren't I okay? Look at me! I don't bother anyone! I am not ugly! I want to be pretty, not healed! I want to be loved, not fixed!*

Discovering Occupational Therapy

When I grow up, I want to go to college. I repeated this refrain to my family often. Other than having that goal, I just wasn't sure what to do.

I didn't know how I could take care of myself in the world. Remembering the wonderful experiences of physical therapy when I was twelve, I decided to study the course work required to enter a physical therapy program.

I realized that after a lot of study, and with great disappointment, I wouldn't be able to perform the physical aspects of physical therapy; it requires lifting, having good balance, and strength that I just didn't have.

So, I looked into occupational therapy. I read in the coursework description that occupational therapists help folks regain their independence in dressing, feeding, and washing themselves. They help folks who have suffered physically or psychologically disabling conditions learn how to prepare a meal, care for a child, or cross a street.

I thought that this was just amazing; this seemed to fall in line with my own strong desire for independence. I also read that occupational therapists deal with the psychology of disability and I recognized this as central to my own healing. I had finally found the profession that I was meant to practice; I *was* occupational therapy.

I've had the privilege of working with thousands of patients over the course of thirty years, but certain patients will always stay with me.

Lipstick Lady

One day, as I was working in an outpatient clinic, I recognized a young woman approaching me. She had a smile that seemed to reach out and land on my own face. Her blue eyes were sparkly with joyful tears and her blond hair glowed around her like a halo. Her joy surrounded her.

I knew her as the daughter of a patient I had treated the year before. Her mom had suffered a profoundly devastating stroke; she had been bed ridden, unable to speak or understand language, and unable to move or care for herself. We had initially met when her mother arrived at our rehabilitation unit.

She had described her mother before the stroke, as a genteel southern woman. She had been loving and outgoing; the epitome of femininity, graceful and ever gracious, a woman proud of her looks, always with hair done, make up on, and flattering clothes. Her mother was proper and well-respected by family and friends. And she was oh-so-loved by her daughter.

By learning about the *woman inside* the patient I saw in bed, I discovered what our treatments would include; I needed to find the key to unlock her from the prison of this stroke.

I would come into my patient's room and speak to her as we went through the motions of combing her hair or washing her face, with my hand guiding her right hand through the motions of these tasks. Sometimes her eyes were open and alert but many times, her eyes were closed.

One day, I saw that her daughter had left lipstick on the nightstand and I wrapped my patient's hand around that wonderful, magical tube of lipstick.

She seemed to awaken; she put the lipstick to her mouth and drew a lovely smile. This was our breakthrough! We connected! We did this daily, but I wasn't able to help my patient make many more gains and she went home with her daughter to live out the rest of her days with family.

Many of us staff wondered how, although her daughter was loving, she could manage to care for a woman who was bed-ridden, non-responsive, and so densely affected by her stroke. We knew that our patient's daughter needed to follow her own conscience and care for her mother as long as she was able, but we took bets on how long she could manage before needing to be hospitalized herself due to over work and over stress.

A year later, when I saw her daughter in the clinic, I was expecting to offer condolences but instead, she greeted me with a big smile and said, "Guess who's here with me," and then I saw a beautiful, tall woman walk in using a cane. This woman had properly coiffed hair, lovely clothing that complimented her complexion, and LIPSTICK. This was her mother!

I wouldn't have even recognized her, and I admit that I was teary upon seeing her. Her daughter asked her if she remembered me from her days in the hospital and, although her mother was gracious and polite, told us that no, she didn't remember me. I expressed my utter joy at seeing her so well and I said goodbye.

It made me feel so blessed to have seen her; I had to remind myself that, yes, every life is meaningful, and every interaction is meaningful.

I saw them again later that week and this lovely

woman who had been my patient, made a point to come up to me. She told me that when I had said goodbye and walked away from her earlier that week, I triggered a memory for her. She had remembered me as the woman with the limp who used to see her in the hospital. She had remembered me as I was limping away from her. I had never been so thankful for my limp before that time.

It gave me chills to realize that a woman I had treated, a woman who was essentially non-responsive, could recognize me as the *woman who limped*.

I was reminded yet again of the power of our words and actions, that they have the potential to not only heal but truly change someone's life even if we are never made aware of those changes. In living a life with love, that love becomes transformative not only in the giving but also in the receiving of love.

Who is Guillain-Barre?

Guillain-Barre is the name of an auto immune syndrome that affects the peripheral nerves in the body; my patient experienced muscle weakness in an unusual manner, first at the center of the body moving outward to her hands and feet. It even affected the muscles of breathing, requiring that she be put on a ventilator.

My patient was placed in a specialized unit within the hospital, an intensive care unit, where only a few open rooms surrounded a central nurses' station. She remained on a ventilator for months.

Treating my patient in an intensive care unit was intimidating due to the amount of machinery and technology she needed to survive; my patient was hooked up to a ventilator, a blood pressure monitor, an oxygen monitor, intravenous medicine, a chest monitor, a urine catheter bag, and finally wrist restraints to keep her from accidentally pulling these tubes out of her body.

There are lots of beeps, hums, and sighs from the machinery, but it is usually very quiet; conversations are subdued, and staff speak quietly to one another, as if in church.

As a therapist working on an intensive care unit, it can be stressful and at times seemingly overwhelming to attempt to manage all the tubes and wires while trying to provide care.

It was imperative that I monitor this machinery to determine if my patient's activity or positioning was harmful to her. I enjoyed working with patients who were on the Intensive Care Units because I believed they received so little normal stimulation, and I was eager to change that.

Any time my patient on the intensive care unit was touched or handled, it was usually uncomfortable or painful. She flinched when touched or pulled away from being touched. My goal was to have my patient comfortable enough to be bathed. I wanted her to use her hands to wash her face even though she was unable to breathe for herself.

This patient was a teenaged girl with severe Guillain-Barre, she was in the intensive care unit, on a respirator, and her prognosis was poor. She and I held hands for a while, my warmth penetrating her cold palm. I guided her hand with a warm washcloth, up to her face. This short task fatigued her greatly, but I kept on seeing her regularly for a month or so until she could sit up in bed for a short while. Then, she left the hospital and I didn't think about her until about a year later.

I was in the grocery store checkout lane, placing my items on the conveyor belt and the cashier looked at my hands and asked if I had worked at the local hospital. I was confused but said yes, that I did still work there. The cashier told me that she recognized the ring on my hand from our work together on the intensive care unit.

I was overjoyed at seeing this lovely, healthy young woman and was so proud to have been a part of her life and her recovery. I felt the warmth of emotion flood through me. She thanked me, but I truly thank her for giving *me* the joy of purpose.

All Cracked Up

Not only did I work in hospitals, I also worked with patients who were too well to be in the hospital but were essentially home-bound because of their pain, immobility, or such low endurance from their condition.

I had the opportunity to work with a young man in his twenties who suffered two broken hips, a broken shoulder blade and some cracked ribs after a motorcycle accident. He had been an active guy and loved spending time outdoors but now he was confined to his home; frequently confined to his bed.

He was married, and his wife was concerned about her husband's ability to care for himself while she was at work during the day. We focused our treatment on being able to get dressed, to get in and out of the bathroom, and to get something out of the fridge.

My patient was in a wheelchair during his healing at home but could stand for a moment or two until his pain limited him. After accomplishing some of the basics of self-care, he spoke to me about how much his wife had done for him, how grateful he was for her, but also how ineffectual he felt. His role as husband and caretaker was non-existent now and I was saddened that he felt like a burden to her.

Rather than just tell him that his wife surely loved him and didn't see him as a burden, we set about exploring how he enjoyed caring for her while appealing to his sense of participating in traditional masculine occupations. He came up with a goal for himself; he would wax his wife's car for her!

We set about strengthening those muscles that

would aid him; we came up with new products and methods to wax her car. We waited for the weekend and we got to work. As I washed and dried the car, he prepared everything he needed to wax her car and he began to work. My heart swelled with pride as I saw the sweat pour off his face; he grunted through his pain and fatigue. It took us several hours, but he accomplished so much more than waxing a car.

We had set out on a journey together, but he had made it to the finish line on his own using every drop of strength and determination he could wring out of himself.

Joy and love communicated itself through his wife's smile and she hugged him gingerly.

Our next session would be our last, I thought, but my patient brought something to my attention. At a lull in conversation during our treatment session, he said that his wife was afraid to touch him. He had trouble looking me in the eye, but I could sense how important this was to him, so we explored this a bit.

It turned out that his wife was fearful of hurting him with hugs and with loving touch. They were also not sleeping in the same bed. My patient also spoke of his prolonged healing of 3-6 months and wanting to be intimate with his wife at some future date.

I realized that by actively listening and allowing him to express his concerns was enough to lower his frustration level and raise his mood. At this point he was able to receive any information I might give, and he was also thinking clearly enough to develop strategies for dealing with these issues.

My initial response was to ask him if he felt comfortable talking to his wife about his concerns and if he wanted me to be a part of the conversation. He replied that I didn't need to speak to his wife just yet, but we set up some new goals for him.

He would learn how to hold his wife, how to spoon together in bed while maintaining good and proper positioning for his healing hips. He would also be educated in positions that were contraindicated for him due to his healing fractures.

He could rebuild his identity as provider, spouse, and lover while decreasing his dependence on his wife.

To help a man regain his sense of self-worth, to help him establish goals for himself, and to give him the tools to reach those goals, that's what being an occupational therapist is all about.

Occupational therapy was a true calling for me, a vocation. It tapped into my inner core beliefs of self-determination and self-actualization. I could live my beliefs while helping others.

Chapter 7

Connecting to My Beautiful

The minute I heard my first love story I started looking for you, not knowing how blind that was. Lovers don't finally meet somewhere, they're in each other all along.

- Rumi

And now we've come full circle; the end of our path is recognized as the starting point. This Beautiful that we all seek a connection to, has been within us all along. Those things and those people that we thought were separate from us are actually to be found within.

This path I've traveled has led me to recognize that throughout history and across cultures, each one of us is connected to the other. Interconnectedness is not something that is achieved but rather is unveiled, discovered, and then acknowledged.

Once acknowledged, this truth allows freedom from the misperception of separateness. This belief in separation leads to limiting concepts of shame, suffering, self-destruction, disgust, fear and depression.

Moving from Shame to Trust and Vulnerability involved being open to those divine moments, those gifts provided, that allow for light and truth. Moving from a perception of aloneness to one of connection allows for growth.

Separation is an ever-present lie hiding the breathtaking and life-giving truth of *trust, hope, self-love, empathy, courage, confidence, and purpose.*

We are all connected through art, music, storytelling, nature, and touch. Our connection reveals a deep-seated knowledge of our responsibilities not only to ourselves but to each other. Thus, the need to reach out to others is merely a reaching in to ourselves.

From this awareness of our interconnectedness springs hope.

Trust

Trust can only be achieved through vulnerability, opening ourselves up to the possible judgement and criticism of others. However, in becoming more vulnerable, we also open ourselves to the transformative power of love. We not only open ourselves to the receiving of love but the giving of love, as well.

Hope

Hope is available to us all because it belongs to everyone; it's in the psyche, the brain, the gut, and the soul. It's inseparable from skin, muscle, bone, blood, cells and even atoms because hope is one of the fundamental building blocks of creation.

By its very nature hope is creation, for in hoping for enlightenment, we create an understanding of it. It's in the seeking that we find our truths.

Hope arising from suffering is brought about through the discovery of meaning in that suffering. That suffering is given value when reframed into the knowledge of connectedness rather than the misperception of suffering as a solitary experience.

Self-Love

Self-destruction can be transformed into self-love not by a solitary exploration but rather through the immersion in all life, including art and nature, as well as other peoples' connection to us, at times thought of as fate. We must learn to value our own journey through the darkness of self-destruction, only then can we recognize the meaning of our lives.

Empathy

Empathy pours forth when self-destruction is given meaning and purpose, it strengthens our bonds to others. It develops when recognizing the suffering of others.

When we recognize the light of empathy that shines forth once we acknowledge that separation from each other does not exist, it is a gift of healing.

Courage

Courage is merely fear acknowledged. Once fear is explored and accepted as a human condition and not a solitary one, courage can flourish. Knowledge of interconnectedness allows for courage because all experiences are shared.

Confidence and Purpose

Finding confidence and purpose is yet another gift we receive when acknowledging connection to others, art and music, words and storytelling, and connection to nature and the universe. Depression arises from the mistaken belief in separateness and isolation.

Connecting to Beautiful, the Divine, Mother Nature, Others. We are all one.

Our calling is to seek, to hope, and to Connect to Beautiful.

Chapter 8

Living in Beautiful

Thank you, dear reader, for joining me on my trek to connect to beautiful.

Now it's time for you to pack up and get started on your path to connect with the Beautiful in your own life. Making those connections with people, with nature, with art and music, and with words and stories, will lead you to Hope and to Beautiful. It's inevitable.

Finding those little sparks of divinity in your own life is such a delight! It's a birthday cake for the soul! The joy of truth and discovery are life changing; meaning and purpose are revealed to each and every one of us.

The revelation comes when we discover that which we had sought outwardly has been waiting patiently inside us. We need only look inside ourselves with love to find our worth and meaning.

We can only look inside ourselves with love by reaching out to others. To discover our interconnectedness, to realize that no one is truly separate, is to recognize the divine plan. We are all responsible to each other as we are responsible to ourselves. That which we do to another, we do to ourselves.

When we honor others, we honor and love ourselves.

I'm newly married; I'm now a mother and grandmother. I'm an author and occupational therapist.

I'm experiencing the heady, happy newlywed joy of having found my soulmate and recently being married for the first time! My having CP and all the accompanying impairments associated with CP seem to be like a soft breeze rather than a gusty wind to him.

His priorities are a reflection of his beliefs – that love will always find a way. He teaches me about perseverance and commitment as well as doing the right thing even when thwarted.

At the age of 54, I find myself a mother to a wonderfully outgoing and outspoken 30-year-old step daughter and to my son-in-law. I also find myself wanting to be the kind of loving and supportive mom that I know my own mother wanted to be for me. We enjoy laughing over shared meals and beach time romps. Listening is now my fall back when there's nothing left to say.

I want to be a part of the grandchildren's busy lives. I wonder if I can have an influence on them; I want to teach them the joys of cooking and eating homemade pizza. I want to show them the magic of constructing a quilt or demonstrate the determination needed to write an uplifting book for children with disabilities.

I enjoy seeing the adolescent mind develop, by being challenged and allowed to grow beyond perceived boundaries. These grandchildren remind me to direct my passions toward the truly important things in life – each other.

Becoming an author has been a journey in and of itself. I find that while I do not enjoy promoting myself, I am dedicated to sharing my message. I've discovered a part of myself that had been forgotten; the striver, the digger, the mover, and the catalyst. I want to be a catalyst for change.

My mission is to educate others about the need to rebuild the life roles (including intimacy) of those people with disabling conditions and to take the time to lovingly educate our children who have disabling conditions. They are important to our future.

For more information about continuing education credits for occupational therapists and nurses, speaking engagements and book signings, or the latest children's book by Deb Drake, please email her at DebDrakeOTR@iCloud.com

Bibliography

Introduction

Mother Teresa (1997).
No Greater Love. New York, NY: MJF Books.

CHAPTER 4

Campbell, Joseph (1988).
The Power of Myth. New York, NY: Knopf
Doubleday Publishing Group.

CHAPTER 5

Kabat-Zinn, Jon (1994).
Wherever You Go There You Are. New York, NY:
Hyperion.

Author Biography

Debra's first memories of rehabilitation came at the hormonally unsound age of twelve, after which she received surgery to aid her mobility.

She promptly fell on, then in love with her physical therapist who shall forever remain unaware of the role he played in guiding her vocation. Her desire to work in rehabilitation remained long after that pivotal moment and she later became an occupational therapist, reaching out to the disabled and helping them to become more independent in their own lives.

She now seeks to dispel the misconceptions about being disabled and emphasizes the commonalities rather than the differences of others.

This is the story of a disabled child becoming a woman and leading a life of joy and beauty.